DISCARDED

MASK OR FACE

REFLECTIONS

IN AN ACTOR'S MIRROR

ALSO BY
MICHAEL REDGRAVE
The Actor's Ways and Means
Mask or Face

KING LEAR

Shakespeare Memorial Theatre

Stratford on Avon, 1953

MICHAEL REDGRAVE

MASK OR FACE

REFLECTIONS

IN AN ACTOR'S MIRROR

HEINEMANN

LONDON MELBOURNE TORONTO

William Heinemann Ltd
LONDON MELBOURNE TORONTO
CAPE TOWN AUCKLAND
THE HAGUE

Published in 1958
Reprinted 1959

© by MICHAEL REDGRAVE 1958
All rights reserved

Printed in Great Britain by
Billing and Sons Limited
Guildford and London

CONTENTS

FOREWORD	11
MASK OR FACE	13
TO BE ME OR NOT TO BE ME	48
SHAKESPEARE AND THE ACTORS	65
ACTORS AND AUDIENCES	92
I AM NOT A CAMERA	120
NOTES ON DIRECTION	149
ECHOS DE CONSTANTIN	171
EPILOGUE	186

LIST OF PLATES

King Lear (*Bryan Heseltine*)   *Frontispiece*
King Lear (*Angus McBean*)   *Facing page* 32
Hector (*Tony Armstrong-Jones*)   32
Harry (*John Vickers*)   33
Rakitin (*John Vickers*)   33
Antony (*Angus McBean*)   48
Shylock (*Graphic House*)   48
The Colonel (*John Vickers*)   49
Philip Lester (*Angus McBean*)   49
Mr Horner (*J. W. Debenham*)   80
Hamlet (*John Vickers*)   80
Baron Tusenbach (*Houston Rogers*)   81
Gilbert (*Gainsborough Pictures 1928 Ltd.*)   96
Kipps (*Twentieth Century*)   96
Alan Mackenzie (*Paramount*)   96
On the set with Cavalcanti (*Ealing Studios*)   97
Orin Mannon (*R.K.O.*)   97

LIST OF PLATES

A visit while on location	*Facing page* 128
Jack Worthing (*Gill*)	129
Andrew Crocker-Harris (*J. Arthur Rank Organization Ltd*)	129
Déliot (*Norman Hargood*)	129
Fowler (*United Artists*)	144
General Medworth (*M.G.M.*)	144
Sir Arthur (*British Lion*)	145
Percy (*British Lion Films Ltd*)	145
What the fans require!	168
Prospero (*Angus McBean*)	169

TO MY WIFE

RACHEL KEMPSON

FOREWORD

TO INAUGURATE the Theodore Spencer Memorial Lectures in 1950, Harvard University invited Mr. T. S. Eliot, who spoke on *Poetry and Drama*. This was, I need hardly say, a lucid and persuasive address; not the less exciting, indeed all the more so, because of its quiet and gentle tone.

As the inaugural lecturer Mr. Eliot gave something more than a formal tribute to the late Boylston Professor of Rhetoric at Harvard, in whose name the lectureship was founded. The lecture and the valediction remain in my mind as a model of how such things on such an occasion should be said and how what is seemingly a sheaf of notes can prove to be much more than a random harvest.

In other years, Mr. Elia Kazan, the director, and Mr. Arthur Miller, the playright, myself as an actor in 1956, and in 1958, M. Michel St. Denis, were invited to speak of our correlated crafts. For my talk I chose the title which now appears on the cover of this book.

In a previous volume of published lectures, *The Actor's Ways and Means*, the substance of which were the Rockefeller Foundation Lectures at Bristol University in 1952-3, I cautioned the reader that my words might perhaps amount to no more than an interim statement and that since the actor's feelings about his craft were now and then subject to change, I could not be certain to feel constant to them in even a year's time. It was an overcautious statement and five years later I find that there is little

FOREWORD

that I want to alter, although of course I can see that much of it might have been better or more clearly expressed.

Five of the chapters of this present book were written as lectures and in revision I have kept to the pattern of a lecture, for that seems to me as convenient and readable a form as the Dialogue or Conversation Piece have proved in other fields of essays and criticism.

For the most part these lectures have been completely revised, word by word. The form and substance, however, are the same as when delivered.

Inevitably, in a collection of pieces written at different times, on the same subject, some of the ideas must overlap and occasionally in seemingly identical manner. I have done my best to iron out these creases, but I am aware that whatever coherence this book may have must come from whatever unity is to be found in the knowledge of the writer, such as it is, or in his way of looking at things.

My thanks are overdue to Mr. Edward Thompson and Mrs. Joan Sparks for their patience and encouragement; also to Mr. Harold Clurman for many quotations and ideas, some received and some, by his permission, borrowed.

Parts of Mask or Face *were first printed in* Encore *and of* I am not a Camera *in* Sight and Sound. Shakespeare and the Actors *is reprinted by permission of Max Reinhardt and Hodder and Stoughton, from* Talking of Shakespeare *edited by John Garrett. The notes on* Directing Uncle Harry *were published in* New Theatre, *as was* The Stanislavski Myth; *the second was reproduced in* Actors on Acting *(Crown Publishers, New York, 1949). The first, revised, forms the preface to the Samuel French acting edition of the play. The notes on Stanislavski and Brecht first appeared in* World Theatre, *Volume IV, No. 1 in 1954. Grateful acknowledgements are made to the publishers and editors.*

LONDON, 1958

MASK OR FACE

FOR THE MOMENT let us forget Eastern Standard, Pacific and even Greenwich Mean Time. For our convenience it is now Curtain Time, or soon will be. In about an hour the curtains in all the theatres of the world will go up. Theatres which don't need curtains will continue not to need them. Theatres which are 'dark,' in the American and vividly poetic sense of the word, will remain dark. I would like to say that I think the dark theatres ache at this moment, but that would be indulging too soon in the pathetic fallacy, so I will restrain myself to what I know. For I am sure that actors on their way to work hurry past a dark theatre.

Some of the actors are already in their dressing-rooms. They don't want to receive visitors now, but I will introduce you to them as if I were Prospero and they spirits. Spirits indeed some of them partly are.

Here is one. A veritable Dybbuk, trying to possess another man's body and mind. On his dressing-table are wigs on blocks, noses in putty or plastic, beards and whiskers, odd bottles and small brushes of all shapes. Two mirrors, at least. The large mirror and the hand mirror. He is as particular as a surgeon about the dressing-table lights. No electrician could ever design a set of lights to satisfy all actors; which is possibly why no electrician ever seems to try. Beside the sticks and tins of Leichner and Max Factor lies the actor's watch. The hands are marching faster than in the earlier hours, it would seem. He is not in a hurry, but lost minutes at this hour fall like shillings in the slot. Minutes gained are worse than worthless, if the curtain is delayed for any length of time, for whatever reason, the actor is as frustrated as he would be if he were behind time himself.

But, of course, he is seldom behind time. This is his 'time of day.' As much his as the sun's at noon. He has been there in his room for an hour before the curtain goes up, probably more. In the mysterious mathematics of the theatre – and in the theatre it is only the agents who understand mathematics – the 'half-hour' means thirty-five minutes and the 'quarter' twenty. 'On stage, please,' which has latterly replaced the quaint 'Overtures and beginners,' means that the spirits have five minutes to strut and fret, or quip and skip down to the stage, according to their mood. And while I am marking time with such apparent trivia, let me mention that the voice of the call-boy, or the voice of an assistant stage manager, relayed over the sound system, requires as careful modulation as the actor gives to his curtain-call. 'Not too eager, not too anxious, never servile, never, never jocose or gloomy' should be the call-boys' or call-girls' signature tune. Incidentally, I once asked one of the world's great violinists how he managed his impeccable 'calls.' He answered without hesitation that he thought 'polite condescension' was the ticket. I think that, for great musicians, he is right. I have seen actors attempt it and fail. With actors, the tragedy lingers on or cheerfulness breaks through too soon. The solo curtain-call is a signature which is as difficult to write as that to an important letter. There must be a most delicate and yet decisive blend of spontaneity and purpose. The purpose is art, the spontaneity craft. It is the same delicate, decisive and difficult task as acting itself, and when it is achieved it all seems easy.

Our actor-spirit is almost on his way to the stage. There is no need for him to run over his words. There would be no time anyway. In any case he has probably thought of the difficult passages during the day. He has rested, probably slept, during the afternoon: the first rule for a long life for those who haunt the evenings. He has got up from his table once or twice during that hour before curtain-time. During these last five minutes one of the mirrors calls him back several times. An hour ago the face in the mirror lost the character of the man in the street or the restaurant and even with the first strokes of his hand became impersonal, androgynous, vague as a map drawn on a handkerchief. Then the muscles of the face started to flex. A deep frown gives way to an almost hostile stare, as if the face in the mirror were saying 'Who are you? What do you want of me?'

With a pencil or brush he gives a last and more decisive stroke. Probably to the eyes, for the eyes are, as it were, the visa to his passport.

Behind him, on the periphery of the mirrors, hovers a shape, his dresser, who may be, if we are on the continent of Europe, a woman. He or she slides in and out of the corners of the mirrors more or less silently. Like all good actors, good dressers have personalities which they can shed – if ever the phrase were valid it is here – at the drop of a hat. They know when to talk and when not to talk. They know when they are wanted and when to disappear. I would like to say they never forget anything. They seldom do. When they do, for them it is a bad performance. These attendant spirits, when they are good, are worth their weight in ticket stubs. When they are not good they may not be horrid but they have to go. Their relationship with the actor is like a long and perilous betrothal. Trust and fear are intermingled.

The dresser gives the actor his hand props, and prepares to

follow him to the stage. On the way to the stage is another mirror where several other actors pause for a moment. Our actor looks into it, a more distant, full-length look. The mirror looks back at him and answers his previous question. 'I want you.'

You find this look in the mirror too fanciful? It is not so to the actor. You find our actor too solemn? Maybe you are right. Those who take art seriously are frequently accused of taking themselves too seriously. Let us look at another mirror, another actor.

* * *

Our next actor has been in make-up all day. At about 8 o'clock this morning he arrives at the film studio, slumps into a barber's chair in the make-up department, rubs his sleepy, newly shaved face with his somewhat trembly hand, scratches his thinning hair in a thatch over his furrowed brow, and with a groan says 'God knows why the public should be expected to want to see that!' The make-up expert laughs at this customary piece of inverted vanity. He thinks our friend the actor is amusing. As indeed he is. He is an institution. His wit appears to be an accepted fact, though nine times out of ten it is more a received idea. He has invented, or acquired and partly purloined, a personality which is very different to that boy who, in the nineteen-twenties, entered in whitish flannels through those repertory french-windows, swinging a tennis racket and exclaiming brightly 'Who's for a knock-up?' At that time this produced only a slight reaction from the audience, except from one stray and astonished American who let out a guffaw and was quickly shushed by the lady in the row in front who always had the same seats the same night each week. This inveterate theatre addict – may whose race perish never! – had already noted the callow young actor. Nor were his gangly, lean, slightly tired, young looks lost on other ladies. No one took him seriously as an actor, least of all the other actors, though even they had to admit that in a really funny part not even he could fail. But that was one of the reasons why he was so well liked in the company: he seemed to offer no serious competition. He never spoke of his ambitions. He didn't seem to have any. His career seemed destined to be a brief and finally disappointing extension of the Oxbridge Amateur Dramatic Society. This would have been predicted, except, of course, by the girls who wrote for his picture, by everyone. Except, again, men of the theatre, like the late William Armstrong of Liverpool, who have flair.

Even he might have been none too sure at first. But he would have noticed before anyone else that the boy worked; that though he had one of the amiably exasperating English habits of running himself down, criticism never appeared to ruffle him; he even seemed to enjoy being a fool; he looked vaguely tubercular but he was in fact as strong as a horse.

In those days people said he hadn't got a brain in his head. Now they say: 'You know, he's no fool.' Nor is he. He has accepted his limitations and decided to make the best of them, which is a sounder recipe for success than vaulting ambition. His success is undeniable. It is even its own guarantee. That name in lights above no matter what title means what the box office calls a solid advance. At the moment it is spread in bold neon letters across the front of a Shaftesbury Avenue theatre, for our actor, after eight or nine hours at the film studio is now about to get ready for the stage. The stage-door keeper has handed him his mail and he shuffles this like an expert card player. The letters posted to the theatre are mostly marked

Personal and are therefore fan mail. The others have been brought to the theatre from his home by his secretary who has pencilled comments and reminders.

The actor drops on to the divan-bed and shuts his eyes. He is so adept at snatching sleep that even the hubbub of Soho around him and the murmurs of a gallery queue outside his window won't prevent him from sleeping. He wakes when the buskers come, performing to the queue. The sound of others performing always alerts him even if he finds small pleasure in what they are doing.

He does not have to think about the performance which lies ahead of him. He has played it several hundred times and will probably play it for several hundred more, in London or on Broadway. What matters at the moment is a responsive house tonight. Given that stimulus and with, possibly, the added stimulus of a non-habit-forming pill or some less dependable potion, he can get through the evening not only comfortably but with ease and authority. It is the thought of the early morning call to the studio which depresses him. But no! Tomorrow is Saturday and he doesn't film on matinée days and British films long ago adopted the five-day week. He doesn't have to do much to change his make-up. Wash off one layer of what passes for flesh colour and substitute another; touch up the eyes a little and it is done. If he gets into his first act suit at the quarter it is time enough. Shall he go up and see the leading lady? No, she doesn't like to be disturbed, except by him. He goes up to say hello and light a cigarette in the dressing-room of an older actress who doesn't come on till forty minutes after the curtain is up. She also adores him but does not, ostensibly, want to possess him.

The actor and the dresser start the business of putting on the suit for the first act. The actor thinks of his first scene for a moment. It's a difficult first scene because its major premise is hard to swallow. Once that is over, the piece runs on its own momentum and the personalities of the actors. It is a piece which will be played in every repertory in England and in summer stock in America for years to come. When it comes to be performed on Broadway it will receive mixed notices and the critic of the *New Yorker* will remark that although the play, as a play, seemed to him Much Ado about Less than Nothing, the actors seemed to enjoy it as much as the audience. This he will express, of course, much more wittily than I have done and it will be an accurate summary; but the play, though apparently pointless, has one point; the point is in the doing of it. It may be a vehicle, but it is a Rolls Royce. A rather old Rolls Royce perhaps, but it streams along.

The English actors will be dismayed when they read that notice. They should console themselves by the words of another American critic who says of this strain of English actors that they are 'disarmingly impudent, self-confident and very modest at the same time. They are entirely immersed in the fine task of being entertaining. They are our humble servants and have a grand time at the job they have taken pains to learn thoroughly.'

As the actor leaves for the stage he stubs out a cigarette. His eye falls on the small pile of neglected correspondence. A buff envelope seems to have seeded itself there. He picks it out gingerly between finger and thumb. It is marked 'On Her Majesty's Service.' With a hollow stage laugh he throws it over his shoulder and when the dresser clucks with amused sympathy the actor says: 'It makes yer laugh, don't it?' But as he jauntily descends the stairs to the stage, he adds, to himself, 'Why do I do it all? I can't keep the money, anyway.'

* * *

At a bistro not far from the Boulevard Clichy sit two young actors. A young actress approaches them. She looks at them and smiles, for from their expressions you would think they shouldered the problems of Europe. 'Come along, you two!' she says. They turn and stare. 'After all,' she adds 'it's time.' One of the boys looks round as if searching vaguely for a clock. He has decided that a watch is bourgeois and pawned it in any case to pay the rent. The other rises with an air of 'Don't let's excite ourselves.'

The three of them saunter along and turn off up a narrow street towards a little box of a place. You would hardly notice it among the restaurant signs and the anonymous-looking fronts of transient hotels. It is their theatre.

As they walk along, their conversation, though desultory, is most likely informed and amusing. But one of the young men is silent. He has decided today that he is a failure, that he ought to have stuck to writing or to being a chemist. He intends to make his silence felt, for he has decided that if he has to be a failure he will be a failure in a big way.

His companions seem oblivious of the shape and size of his despair for they have seen it loom too often. He has too few lines in the play and thinks he should have played the other, his friend's, part. The number of the lines may well seem more important than usual. For none of them appears in the play. They only speak. With the degree of intellectualism of which only the French are capable and that *aboutisme* which they have perfected, these existentialist children are on their way to perform a play in which no character actually appears and where the gimmicky climax, enthralling a sparse but devout audience, occurs when a piece of furniture moves of its own volition.

Small wonder, then, if they seem in no hurry to get to the

theatre. But in spite of the glumness of the third, they are all happy. They are members of the movement known as *Anti-Théâtre*. They 'belong,' and it is a very warm feeling, the feeling that you belong. It may be a Dead End but even a Dead End has its cosy aspects.

The name of their piece and their theatre I do not know. Nevertheless, as a collector of collector's pieces, I would like to think that in March of 1956 I would have hurried to the Théâtre de la Huchette to see M. Jean Tardieu's *Une Voix Sans Personne*, a play in which no one at all appeared on the stage. I admit that the insincerity of this wish is not lessened by the fact that I did not happen to be in Paris.

* * *

In Japan the performance has gone on most of the day. The actor's dressing-room is so plain and spare that even a photograph gives you a whiff of its cleanliness. The make-up on the table is very simple, for it is of the standard colours which the actor was born to use and will die using. The only unusual thing is against a wall: a curious wooden antique object, halfway between a box and a stool. It is a torture block, and it is kept there for reasons more personal to this player than the other symbols in other rooms; the tapestry of first-night telegrams and woollen bunny rabbits. It is a torture block. This grisly fetish is a kind of altar. To this actor, his dressing-room is a private chapel to his church, the theatre. To him, as to the first actor whom we met, his home is something of an hotel.

* * *

In East Berlin the cafés are abuzz with *kaffeeklatsch*, a heady drink brewed by the customers. No one discusses the message of tonight's play by Herr Brecht; or if they do it is in newspaper clichés. For they know the message. It is their own message. Their daily bread. Besides, who wants the message of a play anyway? A play is a statement, or a prayer, or a credo. Tonight's play is the first and the last of these. Its interest lies not in what it says but how it says it. That is how it should be, and how, through the long life of drama, it has been. Shakespeare, we have been repeatedly told, is a second-rate intellect. Ibsen and Shaw remain alive only at their least urgent.

In this theatre we are not in a church, though the audience are the converted. We are in the agora.

* * *

West, by thousands of miles, of East Berlin, at a theatre on Broadway, a first-night curtain is soon to rise and a popular star, who has faced more first nights in rather more varied rôles than fall to the lot of most actors in North American latitudes, is disturbed by angry sounds from Shubert Alley and flustered conversations outside his dressing-room door. He asks, with a testy calm, whether someone will please tell him what is going on? His dresser returns, followed by the stage director who assures him that there is nothing to worry about. Then why, he asks them, are they looking so worried? The stage director tells him that the show is being picketed by the American Legion. The actor turns from the mirror and lifts his eyebrows, conveying infinite bewilderment. A small-part actor in the show, it appears, was once 'named' as a 'liberal.' He has been out of work for some time. The management had thought that the trouble had blown over and remembering his fine work for the Group Theatre in the 1930s had taken the risk; after all, what had he done but attend a few 'Communist front' meetings? The stage director leaves, saying with a bright smile, which he knows to be hollow, 'Don't worry!' The actor does not reply. There is too much ahead of him to worry. He pictures the first-night audience, huddling in the small lobby, trying to shake off their embarrassment at crossing a picket line. Perhaps a few of them, certainly his friends, will sense the unfairness of the situation and give him an extra large 'hand' on his appearance. Perhaps he had better go up and see the other actor and tell him not to worry; that he's a bloody good actor, that it's a damn shame, that it makes no difference... But before he goes he turns to the mirror and says: 'Why did they have to do this to *me*?'

* * *

A mile or so away, in downtown Manhattan, in a building for which 'barn-stormers' would have apologised, gathers a small but ardent audience to see the latest offering 'in the round.' It is Broadway's most successful season, it is said, for twenty years. Arthur Miller, Tennessee Williams, Giraudoux and Thornton Wilder are 'packing them in' all around Times Square. *My Fair Lady* has just opened and it is predicted that it will run through the next war, if there are any theatres left by then. For the theatres are toppling right, left and centre; or simply mouldering into disuse. Such is the absurdity of prices that a theatre which could gross over thirty thousand dollars a week cannot be reopened because its water tank burst and flooded the auditorium. In the past ten years the little 'off-Broadway' theatres have multiplied, some of them have flourished and a few of them have even become 'smart.' New and exciting reputations have been launched. To the American actors, of whom over ninety per cent are unemployed, the 'off-Broadway' theatres are a godsend. Not that there are enough new little theatres to support more than a small fraction of the actors. But they help to keep alive their hope, and actors need a lot of hope. The schools of acting also help to keep it alive, and it is safe to say that in New York there are more schools of acting than there are theatres.

After the show, at midnight, some of them will be going to an acting class, for in no city in the world is there such a craving for instruction. In the morning, hundreds of them, dressed more for the waterfront than for Sardi's, will attend acting classes up and down the city, whether they are in work or not. It gives a certain cachet to be in work, of course, but being in class is, perhaps, more classy.

It would take a better pen than mine, and an American pen, too, to describe the glowing faith of these young people; their industry, their vitality, their naïveté; their *schwärmerei* for the latest idol, their cynicism about the latest failure. One feels cynical oneself when one thinks that if one in twenty of them is ever going to be allowed to use in the professional theatre what he has learnt in class this morning it will be a remarkable event. It would be cruelty to point out that Julie Harris and Marlon Brando would have been fine actors anyway, whatever class they had or had not attended.

* * *

That brief stop in New York has already, you will observe, put me in a disputatious mood. In New York everything theatrical is disputed fiercely, accepted values challenged daily or by the hour. It would seem therefore a convenient if not a logical point to stop and consider where this theatrical trip round the globe is leading us. It is an erratic and arbitrary route that we have taken and the stopping places I have deliberately plotted as points on a personal graph. But what is this graph meant to show? I chose a title for this lecture which is vague and atmospheric and personal because I knew that what I wanted to talk about was the question of styles in acting both nationalistic and individual. I could not hope in so brief a space and with my limited knowledge to do more than dabble in the subject. The subject is in any case so fluid and transitory. In these brief sketches I have attempted to suggest the background and conditions in which various actors work and each one of them could perhaps be profitably expanded into a chapter, for before coming to any fair definition of what an interpretative artist is trying to achieve we should consider, as indeed every author must consider, the type of audience to whom he is trying to speak.

It is of course dangerously easy to generalise about style and I can think of only two considerations which are basic to all styles. The first is that there is no one style which is capable of giving full expression to all plays. That is obvious. What is not so obvious is that with actors more than with other artists, faults often stem directly from merits. The English have their excessive originality, which Coquelin noted; an empiricism and individuality which can produce flashes of lightning, like Kean in Shakespeare, on a murky day; the Jews have a coruscating fluidity which can end by stupefying like a fountain, an excess which can first embrace and then smother and which sometimes cries on your shoulder; the French have a precision with which they tend to cut themselves and you; the Italians a surface vitality and a brilliant talent for *verismo*, which does not always conceal an inner lack of true, simple feeling; the Germans insist on dotting their i's and crossing their t's. And in that sentence I cannot have left one American unscratched, for in America nearly all these virtues and vices are inextricably woven, or rather casseroled, or scrambled together with Spanish and Russian and every other race whom I have forgotten or am too ignorant to mention. But before anyone is affronted, let me caution him that I intend by these rough and ready statements to indicate only the tendencies of nationalistic faults. For there are fastidious Jewish actors, so fastidious sometimes that they seem to be rebelling against their racial exuberance; English actors in whom understatement does not preclude passion; French actors, like Raimu, who combine technique with the gifts of a natural; Italians like Duse – I must continue to name only those who are dead – with tumultuous feelings and a simple clear truth like the light of dawn. In fact there are actors and actors, the good ones and the bad ones, the world over.

* * *

When an actor speaks or writes about his craft it is difficult to avoid the impression that he may think that all other actors should model themselves on him. If you have not already read of them, some of my prejudices must have begun to be apparent today. Clearly, I have much sympathy with the kind of actor who is, as the French say, more *comédien* than *acteur*, who is able to change himself in appearance and style to suit the needs of each play. But I would like you to understand that I have the greatest admiration for a few performers who adapt each part and play so that somehow they seem to have been written expressly for them.

In some lectures of mine which have been published, I have tried to pay tribute to what have been called 'Protean' actors; the ones who, like myself, prefer that every part is to some extent a character part. But I have to agree with that fine actor, Mr. Arthur Kennedy, who the other day is reported to have said that the hardest thing of all is to be oneself on the stage. Furthermore,

I would like to correct an impression which I seem to have made previously and assert now that I do not believe and never have believed that the greatest performances are those in which the actor becomes totally unrecognisable. In the higher reaches of the actor's art, the unmistakable stamp of an actor's personality or genius is always to be detected through whatever mask he has created for himself. Irving unmistakably remained Irving and Olivier, though frequently physically unrecognisable for several minutes, remains Olivier.

This leads us to what for centuries – indeed since the time when the nature of acting was first discussed – has been the heart of its mystery. The crux of the paradox. Is it mask or face? I had better say at once that in my opinion the two cannot be separated.

In a sense it is true that the hardest thing of all is to be yourself on the stage. I remember many years ago Edith Evans saying to me 'I envy some of you young people who seem to start off your careers at the very outset with a personality of your own. It took me years to find mine, peeling off layer after layer of myself like an onion until I found the essence.' I was mystified at the time, for I knew that even from her first appearances she was said to have possessed remarkable authority. But I know now exactly what she meant for I have been through the same processes myself. And what she meant was not, of course, the persona which the public and her friends knew, for we all of us, whether we know it or not, have more than one of these, but the essence of her emotional experience and the residuum of a life's philosophy. This is the actress's Face. The rest, her appearance, her voice, her technique, her mannerisms, are the Mask, but without the perfect discipline of the latter, the former would not be visible to us.

* * *

Here in America a school of acting has recently come into being and it is usually referred to as the Method, though there have been other, more derisory, appellations. It derives, through various interpreters and teachers, through its present manifestation in the Actors' Studio, back through the Group Theatre of the thirties, to its chief source of inspiration, Stanislavski. It is usually associated with the names of some of your finest young actors and actresses of today and it seems to me that there is a danger that it will be thought that all that is best in the Method has only just been thought of. Indeed, the historian of the Group Theatre, Mr. Harold Clurman, asserts that 'some of the most significant successes of recent years (1945-55), *A Streetcar named Desire, Death of a Salesman, Member of the Wedding, Teahouse of the August Moon*, to mention only a few, were directed by men whose careers began with the Group. Such actors and actresses as Marlon Brando, Eli Wallach, Julie Harris, Kim Stanley, Maureen Stapleton and Uta Hagen, who never were members of the Group itself, may be fairly claimed as the Group's offspring.'[1]

I would agree with that claim, for I can see little difference in either quality or style between some of these players and the style of, say, Mr. John Garfield and Miss Sylvia Sydney or some of the other leading members of the Group Theatre whether on stage or film. Indeed, some of the best performances of Mr. Brando and Miss Harris and the others have been moulded by Mr. Harold Clurman and Mr. Elia Kazan.

I have said 'all that is best in the Method' and that infers that I consider there are some things which are not so good. Fortunately, however, the worse manifestations of these only seem to

[1] *The Fervent Years* by HAROLD CLURMAN (Hill and Wang, New York, 1957).

apply to the less renowned members of the Actors' Studio, some of whom, one must hasten to add, may be tomorrow's chief glowers.

I will confine myself to saying that, though the Actors' Studio may be an excellent workshop, some of the methods and exercises which have been useful in class are paralysing and destructive and, not to put too fine a point on it, a damn nuisance in the theatre. Mr. Lee Strasberg, the principal of the Actors' Studio, believes with Stanislavski that the actor's work on himself must precede the actor's work on his rôle. This seems logical enough but it is too frequently forgotten that Stanislavski maintained (and all good instinctive actors have always assumed) that the truth of a rôle can be found in the doing of it and that we need not necessarily, and indeed only in rare cases, stop to find the truth of feeling before attempting to portray it. The essence of Stanislavski's teaching in fact is that it helps you to know what to do when your instinct tells you that something is false.

Mr. Strasberg has written that 'some present-day theories of acting suggest that the actor's creative processes differ for different styles of plays, that while one approach may be right for the realistic play, another is necessary for the classic or poetic play.'[1]

In contradiction to this theory he quotes the examples of an ancient Greek actor who 'felt it necessary' to carry on the urn containing the ashes of his dead son when he was to deliver a funeral oration and of a Japanese actor whose theatre was 'dedicated to formal results,' who was made by his teacher to

[1] *The Paradox of Acting* by DENIS DIDEROT and *Masks or Faces* by WILLIAM ARCHER: Introduction by LEE STRASBERG (Hill and Wang, New York, 1957).

walk for hours in the snow in his bare feet in order to prepare him for his rôle. He infers that the type of work to which the Actors' Studio is dedicated does not alter from one style of play to another. He adds that the basic problem of the actor is constant through the ages. 'He is the only artist whose raw material is himself.' There, to my mind, seems to lie his fallacy. Flaubert's 'Madame Bovary c'est moi' is the line to remember. The actor cannot work on himself without relating himself to the author's text any more than Flaubert could create without his knowledge of nineteenth-century provincial society. Flaubert was right, of course, and I think Mr. Strasberg has got the wrong end of the stick. Stanislavski, with his 'the actor's work on himself' also postulated the actor's work on the rôle. Unhappily, too many of Mr. Strasberg's pupils seem to believe that the actor's work begins and ends in himself.

* * *

There are, of course, many actors, directors and producers in New York who know only too well that the actor's work on himself, however subjective or not it may be, is very little help in finding a style for certain kinds of plays. They know that detailed realism is no help at all in Shakespeare and know that the attribute of a good and flexible voice added to clear diction does not preclude sincerity and truth of feeling. But they are in the minority. There are many effective and commanding voices in the American theatre but it would be difficult to name many actors who, like Mr. Orson Welles, Mr. Louis Calhern or Mr. Edmond O'Brien, could fill a theatre with rich, rolling and varied sound. I take leave to doubt, for instance, that Mr. Marlon Brando, fine actor that he is and who by general consent made a good shot at Marc Antony in the film of *Julius Caesar*, could have got away with it without the help of the microphone and the frequent 'cutting' in his long speeches.

To sum up, I think that the present manifestation of the Method is admirable for certain kinds of realistic plays, but I think the onus of the proof of Mr. Strasberg's theory rests with him and that he and his disciples must produce professional productions of plays from Shakespeare, Restoration Comedy or, say, Giraudoux or almost any of the later French playwrights.

Let me add that I am sure that though we have a number of English actors who are highly skilled at realistic acting, we have many more who could find much benefit from certain aspects of the Method. How much I would care to see more and more realistic plays is another matter. Frankly, I would not. And I do not count Mr. Tennessee Williams and Mr. Arthur Miller as realistic playwrights. Their plays contain elements of realism, of course, but essentially much symbolism, and in the lax sense of the word, poetry. Incidentally, I was astonished to find on reading the printed text of *A View from the Bridge* that Mr. Miller, who on this platform objected to poetry in some modern poetic plays as a kind of decoration, printed some of his own lines as if they were verse.

However, play writing is not really within the scope of my theme except in so far as the writing of new plays can affect styles of acting. I will say no more than that to me realism in the theatre is only suitable for melodrama and is not essential to that; that it is a dead-end which has already been explored as fully as the theatre can explore it and that any further developments in realistic acting styles may safely be left to the cinema – where indeed most of the brightest lights from the Actors' Studio of New York sooner rather than later find themselves. Meanwhile, I would suggest to real playwrights – that is, those who wish to write for the theatre – that they take a leaf out of Mr. Tennessee Williams' book and also from the modern French dramatists and see what happens when they try to make life look like the theatre and not the theatre like life. To be sure, plays like *The Middle of the Night* by Mr. Paddy Chayevski achieve excellently as much as they set out to do. But I agree with the American critic who wrote that Chekov's frustrated souls were saints and poets compared to the nice people of *The Middle of the Night*.

* * *

It is neither saint nor poet which has been the aim this evening of our first-mentioned actor, rather how like an angel 'in apprehension! How like a God!' But from the start of the first scene, be it *Hamlet* or *King Lear*, he has no thought of his rôle in terms of gods or angels, but rather of 'What a piece of work is a man!' Yet the picture we take away with us will be over life-size. Take it for all in all, much more than a man.

He waits in the wings for his first entrance, trying as much as possible to keep out of earshot. But he knows the words so well:

'I thought the King had more affected the Duke of Albany than Cornwall.'

A typically difficult opening, this, to a play so universal in scope, so domestic in detail. Granville-Barker remarks that 'Shakespeare had come to prefer this to the grand opening.' But it would seem to have escaped Barker's notice that all the openings of the great tragedies start on notes of doubt and questioning. The opening line of *Othello* is Roderigo's 'Tush, never tell me!' 'Tush, tush,' says Horatio, 'Twill not appear.' Demetrius and Philo in *Antony and Cleopatra* start their brief colloquy with 'Nay, but this dotage of our general's O'erflows the measure.' Sampson and Gregory in *Romeo and Juliet* play a protracted

HECTOR in *Tiger at the Gates*: Apollo Theatre, London: and Plymouth and Helen Hayes Theatres, New York: 1955.

KING LEAR, with Yvonne Mitchell: Shakespeare Memorial Theatre, Stratford on Avon, 1953.

Above, RAKITIN in *A Month in the Country,* with Valerie Taylor: St James's Theatre, 1943. *Right,* HARRY in *Uncle Harry,* with Rachel Kempson: Garrick Theatre, 1944.

game of verbal chess, and the three witches in *Macbeth* never cease questioning each other.

Our actor listens to the sound of the opening lines. 'They've missed it again' he thinks to himself. At the rehearsals the director had suggested to the actors who open *Lear* with this prose passage that their chief concern should be to suggest a private conversation, perhaps whispered, for they are expecting interruption. They have been cautioned to avoid at all costs making exposition sound like exposition. For surely it was written so. This short opening passage was deliberately muted to throw into relief the splendour or mystery of his chief characters' first appearance. But tonight the same mistaken sense of 'giving the play a good start' by 'lifting it' is at work again as can be seen at almost every performance and production of *Hamlet* or *Lear*.

This irritates our actor as he listens in the wings and he slips away from his attendant courtiers who are waiting with him for his entrance. He wonders why English actors, so patient and cunning in understatement in modern plays, are so prone to over-emphasis in the dark corners of Shakespeare's chiaroscuro. When he enters he is tempted to pitch his own opening lines a little lower than usual, in order to make some kind of contrast. It is not how he or the director planned it, but in the rough and ready joinery of the theatre, it may fit.

He does not have time to wonder, though he might well do so, whether they do not order these things better in France or Germany where there would be, in such a theatre as this, a *sous-régisseur* watching the plays every night. He might also agree at this moment with the American director who had said to him that nothing had put so many people off Shakespeare as 'the Shakespeare voice'; for it is true that a large empty voice, full of power but empty of meaning, though it may for a time enforce attention, eventually brings about, by the law of diminishing returns, stupefaction and boredom. And there are too many actors who, when confronted with the wide spaces and sometimes faulty acoustics of the larger theatres, fall too easily into the school of 'when in doubt, shout.'

However, tonight's play, be it *Hamlet* or *Lear*, has played well and, at the end, there is an ovation. If it is an ovation of what might be called the English kind, the actor will not be surprised or disappointed. An ovation is, after all, an ovation. 'The actor needs applause,' said Irving.[1] 'It is his life and soul when he is on the stage. The enthusiasm of the audience reacts upon him. He gives them back heat for heat . . . ' What Irving did not add, but which his grandson Laurence Irving permits me to reveal, and which he would have revealed himself in his superb biography of his grandfather if he had stumbled upon the information in time, was that Irving skilfully had the kettledrummer in his orchestra pit trained to swell the applause when in that gradual way which befits a tragedy it reached its height. This, though it may raise a cynical smile, has my wholehearted and unqualified approval. Whatever means may be employed to increase the pleasure of the public, even if those means include trickery, are justifiable.

Our actor is, as I said, not downhearted because of his 'English' ovation, the kind of ovation which does not bring an audience to its feet: the customary tribute in the continental theatre. For English audiences more than recompense by their long and warm-hearted loyalty to their actors for any lack of heat in their nightly applause. And if our actor is, as he happens to be tonight, feeling curiously flat as he starts to put on his street clothes, it has nothing to do with all this, nor is his deflation a regular nightly

[1] *Henry Irving* by LAURENCE IRVING (Faber and Faber, 1951).

occurrence. But tonight, after the last visitors have gone and he has dismissed the dresser, he lingers for a few minutes and he feels so empty that it occurs to him, not for the first time, that he well understands the turbulent Kean's desire to instruct his coachman to whip his horses towards a brothel in Deptford. He is a disciplinarian both in himself and to others. But the final descent of the curtain is sometimes to him a descent to the brink of Avernus. If he does not descend further it is possibly because he knows from experience that the re-ascent is so painful. However, he dismisses his car and says he will walk home to get some air into his lungs. Like most of us when he is dissatisfied with himself he transfers some of his annoyance on to others and as he strides along the street – where he is almost unrecognised since the evening has left him in a curiously anonymous state – he makes a few mental notes of things that he will mention to the stage director before the next performance of the play. His Horatio – or it may be his Kent – is an actor whom he particularly wished to have in his company, rather as Irving used to like having William Terris. He is a sound, attractive actor of much warmth and stability, but with these qualities goes a little insensitivity. His performances vary as little as do his good looks and his robust strength. Such actors are worth their weight in gold and only debase themselves when they try to excel themselves. Fortunately, as often as not it is part of their temperament to be calm, modest and unambitious. They may suffer pangs of dissatisfaction occasionally but jealousy does not seem to be in their nature. They are adored by the ladies in the audience and loved by their fellow workers. They are conscientious craftsmen, but there is little inspiration or spontaneity.

Suddenly our actor realises the absurdity of this transference of emotion. He reminds himself how lucky he is to have his old friend in the company. He even wonders if he is not being a little jealous of a man who seemingly goes through none of his own tortures and uncertainties, exaltations and 'descents to Avernus.' He wonders whether the ideal actor might not be compounded of their two temperaments.

'There is no such thing as an ideal actor!' he mutters as he hails a taxi and is driven home.

* * *

Holland is a small country with only just enough potential playgoers to keep its municipal theatre companies in existence. Salaries are low and if a production can be played for as many as seventy times it is considered a smash hit. The programme at each of the six or seven municipal theatres is changed nightly and a play is seldom, if ever, given two consecutive performances. This means that each theatre company has to double around the country, travelling between one large town and the other. The Amsterdam company, for example, will play the weekend in their own home base, for the weekend is considered the best time for business, but the rest of the week they will take one or more of their productions to The Hague or Utrecht or both. The mere thought of having to pack and unpack one's make-up and small personal effects two or three times a week is not really made less oppressive by comparing these actors with the strolling players of old. 'Strolling players' is a romantic-sounding title and I have known old actors wax lyrical about 'fit-up' companies, just as those who have spent many a year in weekly repertory are inclined to state that that is the one true way to learn your business. It is nothing of the kind. I have met few actors or actresses who have been subjected to long bouts of weekly repertory whose sensitivities have not become blunted and whose knowledge of their business can be called anything but rough and ready.

The Dutch actors, and the Danes for that matter, are born into a world where several bleak facts stare them in the face. Not only the fact, which is common to most nations, that there are usually more people wanting to act than there are sufficient people wanting to pay to see them do so, but that their mother-tongues happen to be the two very languages which their fellow-Europeans will not bother to learn. Occasionally, very occasionally, a Dutchman or a Dane has succeeded in making a living on the English or the American stage, to be the envy if not the pride of his fellow countrymen. The others know with a fair degree of certainty that international fame and fortune will never be theirs and that their life will contain more bus journeys than would fall to the lot of anyone except bus drivers. Perhaps it is the early recognition of this hard and parochial existence which strengthens the character and the dependability of the Dutch and the Danish. It is easy to speak of the camaraderie of the theatre. These actors must have true camaraderie or perish. They must have, too, a strong sense of dedication and purpose to keep their spirits alive.

The bus from The Hague to Amsterdam rolls through the darkness along the cobbly, straight road. To the right some kilometres and five minutes away are a few dim lights which belong to the small town of Leyden, where Rembrandt was born. But our Dutch actor has seen these so often that the road past Leyden only helps to lull him to sleep. Presently they come to Schipol, the airport of Amsterdam, with its bright lights. Some of the company in the bus are awake and chatting excitedly.

The company have worked together for so long that they know nearly everything there is to be known about each other and, as usual in such cases, intense quarrels as well as great friendships have come into being. But these quarrels will perhaps end in better relations than the enmities and jealousies and internecine feuds which have helped to destroy other companies in other countries. There is, for there has to be, a family feeling. There is also the feeling that 'if this breaks up, what else is there?' These are the terms on which our actor entered the theatre and though from time to time he rebels against his fate, he has long since contented himself to accept it without grumbling and with dignity.

I once knew an elderly Dutch actor in Amsterdam who explained that whatever his troubles might be, and he had had a hard life, especially during the Occupation, he would die happy if he could keep 'his "little box" on the Leidseplan.' He meant his dressing-room in the Stadsschouburg, the municipal theatre on the square.

Some of the actors will go to an Arts Club in Amsterdam and drink and gossip with their Amsterdam friends until the early hours. Our actor seems to be asleep, though in fact he is listening to their conversation. He thinks to himself maybe he had better go to bed when he gets to the town. On the other hand, after a short doze in the bus he will probably wake up and feel like joining them.

* * *

In New York a big party is being given in the Dante Room at the D'Annunzio Hotel. The leading actor has had too many first nights not to know that in spite of the sincere compliments about his performance the evening has been a disaster. Whether the audience would have been so out of key without the prelude of the picketing in the street is something with which at the moment he simply cannot concern himself and it bores him to have it analysed by his agent or other good friends, however well intentioned. The play is over and as far as he is concerned it might as well close tomorrow. It probably will. He is just wondering whether the M.G.M. picture which, in spite of a lot of money, he turned down in order to do this play in which he believed, is still uncast, when the press-agent comes in with the advance news of the leading morning paper notices. He catches his eye and before the press-agent has time to speak the actor makes his swift adieux. 'You poor dear!' says someone. 'After that terrific performance you must be dead!' He gives one of his wonderful, knowing, ambiguous smiles. 'Don't you want to stay and see the notices?' someone else calls out. 'I'll probably pick them up on my way home.' He passes a night news-stand and buys one of the two leading papers. After a glance he folds it and a few yards later drops the paper into a municipal refuse basket. Back in his hotel, after a short, stiff nip of Scotch whisky, and after climbing into bed and taking a couple of sleeping pills, the sad but wise old bird falls quickly and soundly asleep.

* * *

Not more than twenty blocks away a distraught wife has put her husband to bed. He is the actor on whose account the picket-line was formed. A few friends remain, clutching beers or coffee.

'I still think,' says one of them vehemently, 'that you can't deprive a man of his means of living without giving him unemployment benefit! For God's sake . . .'

'For God's sake, shut up! The poor bastard wants to act as much as he wants to live!'

* * *

Our Shaftesbury Avenue actor was feeling as fresh as paint by the end of Act 2 and his leading lady had given one of her more sparkling performances. 'Most actors' says Bernie Dodd in Clifford Odets' play *Winter Journey* (*The Country Girl*) 'don't need four weeks' rehearsing. They repeat the same glib, superficial patterns they found the first or second week. The usual actor gives himself small aims – or the director does it for him. In a couple of weeks they're fulfilled. And it all fits into a small, dull peanut shell.' Our friend's leading lady is one of these. Expert and sharp she may appear to be, alluring certainly, but her performance rarely varies by a hair's breadth. On this she prides herself and it might well seem a matter for congratulation. Unfortunately she has never sought or found or been led to the path of what might dully be called self-improvement because by nature she abhors the difficult. She has never learnt to play to her fellow actors, to listen to them as if each phrase were being said for the first time. No matter how her partner may deliberately vary his performance in order to put a spark of real spontaneity into hers, she clings with an animal obstinacy to the way she has always done it. Tonight, however, two things have happened to her which have given her such exhilaration that she acts with a kind of abandon and generosity which is not usually at her command. As a result, our actor, on whom the play chiefly rests, has surprised even himself in variety and invention. A bit of business which had never occurred to him before has been spontaneously, dazzlingly performed. Even at the moment of accomplishing it, a small mentor in his mind whispers to him: 'You'll never be able to do that so well again.' And his whole performance has seemed so richly in character (which in his case means true to himself) that the audience leaves the theatre purring with delight, except for the occasional congenital dissenter who feels obliged to say 'Of course, the whole thing wouldn't exist without him.'

On the strength of this unexpected Friday night efflorescence, he has asked her, in the second interval, to sup with him after the show. There is nothing she would like more, she says. But returning to her dressing room she finds a telephone message that indicates, to cut a short story shorter, that it may well be to her professional advantage to sup elsewhere. A film producer has 'an interesting idea.'

At the end of the last act, then, our exhilarated actor finds himself suddenly deflated by her profuse apologies. She cannot sup with him and she does not tell him the real reason for she does not wish to wound his vanity. She invents a mysterious ailment and succeeds in wounding it more.

However, as luck will have it, he has a visitor after the play: a distinguished director at one of our two theatres which, for lack of a real one, we call National. Well known for his unconventional approach to the classics the director suggests that our friend might be intrigued by the consideration of playing Malvolio in *Twelfth Night*. He is a very plausive man and his outline of the character of Malvolio based on the well-known silhouette of this popular star would intrigue anyone as an idea. But the name which is gilt-edged security in lights is not so easily caught. He maintains that he has never seen the play and hasn't read it since he was at school when he played Maria. But he will read it tomorrow before the matinée and telephone on Monday or at the latest Tuesday morning.

His aggrievement with his leading lady is forgotten in a matter of moments. It is with a jaunty air that he descends from his car and walks up the steps of the Kemble Club to which, though a member of some standing, he is an infrequent visitor. The admired pictures by Zoffany oppress him with their rigid lay-figures which do not look like actors so much as people pretending to look like actors. When he looks at the pictures at all he prefers those by the minor artists such as Clint, who portray the world of the stage as he sees it, in a fluid motion. His reason for coming to the Kemble is that he has remembered he was invited in to the tail-end of a private dinner party in the Siddons Room. He had almost forgotten the invitation but at this moment it seems opportune.

He is warmly welcomed, and among the usual mixture of medicos and barristers he notices a confrère, a bearded theatrical Knight. Sir Hubert is charmingly suffused with mellow authority and port. Our friend wishes to dodge professional shop-talk but that is not usually possible in the company of Sir Hubert who, with more curiosity than interest, insists that everyone is eager to know what our successful film star and Shaftesbury-Avenue-actor is going to do at the end of the present run, if it ever ends.

This has a freezing effect at the moment, for the younger man has a truly professional contempt for talking about his future plans in public. But the opportunity cannot be missed and he sends up a *ballon d'essai*.

'This'll make you laugh your head off, old boy, but can you see me as Malvolio?'

A curious, indeed inquisitive, pause.

Explanations follow and Sir Hubert, biding his time, delivers an interim statement.

'Interesting! Very. You want to do it?'

'Don't know. That's why I asked you.'

'Oh, *very* interesting! I'll be there on the first night.'

Murmurs of assent from mellow gentlemen not all of whom

can remember on the spot in which play Malvolio appears. Encouraged by this, but truly modest, and, indeed, diffident when off his home ground, the younger actor says: 'Well, I mean, I'm a bit of a non-starter in the Bard or the Canon or whatever he's called.'

Sir Hubert draws his breath in slowly and one cannot be sure whether he is easing his indigestion or his feelings.

'Ah yes' he says, and his voice seems to boom a little more than usual. 'Ah yes, the Old Boy has a way of finding us out.'

* * *

At the bistro near the Boulevard Clichy our young chemist manqué has been in conversation with another actor, a man whose face earns him from time to time employment in the film studios. It is a strange, tired face, deeply lined. It was during a day's work at the studios that he met his young friend. He tells him that he was speaking with the director of a new theatre movement known as Théâtre du Peuple, a vigorous, intellectual man, a popular actor, a good organiser and a born leader. A young member of his company has fallen seriously ill and a replacement is quickly needed. It is suggested that the young chemist-actor would do himself no harm by asking to give an audition.

'What's the good? They'll probably have hundreds there, if he hasn't cast it already!'

'There's never any harm in trying. I think he's got something with that theatre of his. Something that catches the public's imagination, anyway, and he's got some very good actors. What you need is to work in a good company with an exciting director. Better still, to work in a company like that, which has also got an idea behind it.'

The young tragedian pouts a little. 'It's not a very new idea, bringing the classics to the masses. What is there in that?'

'It may not be very new but it's one very few have succeeded in doing in the last thirty years.'

'Seriously, do you like all that stuff, all that posturing and rhodomontade?'

'If you are asking me do I like it when it's badly done, then of course I don't. But when it's well done! . . . If you ask me do I truthfully enjoy some of Corneille and Racine and our insipid translations of Shakespeare, then I will tell you I don't, as such. For me there have been no real tragedies since the Greeks, and that is because of history, not because there have been no great writers. But those fellows, even if they didn't write true tragedies, wrote plays that *work*, that still have power to move an audience on the stage and which, above all, give actors wonderful parts, wonderful opportunities.'

'Yes, but you have to have something of the *cabotin* to get away with those parts. I hate all that.'

'Call it *cabotin* if you like; but to me, who can just remember Mounet-Sully's famous cries as Oedipus, I would rather compare it to Michelangelo lying on his back on the high scaffolding of the Sistine Chapel painting the figure of Adam, that huge figure which from the ground below seems the epitome of the male form. You have to do something comparable in order to be able to play Oedipus or King Lear. The finished result must show no trace either of where the scaffolding was or of the years of preparation or of the tears and the frustrations. The finished performance must be all mankind in one man.'

'Yes, that's all very nicely put and I know what you mean. But don't you think that the essence of acting is the actor's own personality? I mean, in the end doesn't it boil down to that?'

'Of course it does, if by personality you mean that mixture of the spirit and the mind and the feelings – none of which, in any case, can be separated. Yes, in the end, we judge a player by what he is, even though what he is is the strangest mixture, an extraordinary compound of conflicting impulses and so on and so on. But how does that alter my case?'

'Because it seems to me that these days it is not the enlargement of the personality that we are wanting; all that is only spreading it out or blowing it up like a balloon. What we need is the rarefaction of the personality – distillation if you like. You talked of the epitome of mankind in one man. I am content with the essence of the individual.'

The older actor's eyes light up. 'Yes, I know only too well what you mean. I see it every day. Every time I go to the movies – which is seldom. But for how long are you content to see the same facets of the same individual? And, begging your pardon, I do not believe in the essence of the individual. I not only do not believe that there is such a thing but I believe it is wrong to believe that such a thing exists – except of course as a loose phrase just as one might say of someone "That's typical of him!" In fact, my dear young friend, don't start me talking on the blasphemies of Existentialism. I have nothing more to say about it than that I believe it to be one of the Circles of Hell.'

There is a silence.

'You think I should go along, then, tomorrow morning and ask for an audition?'

'As I say, it can't do you any harm. I imagine you could use a job and if you get it you can learn something from that man and from those plays. You were speaking about the essence, just now, about a distillation of a personality. In acting such a distillation is brought about by learning to select, learning how to discard, learning how to sacrifice nine small effects for the sake of one bigger one.'

'Yes, yes, but all that's only to do with good taste. There have been great actors, surely, with no taste at all?'

'I won't agree with you there. It is true that some of the great ones, Bernhardt for one, could descend from the sublime to the vulgar in a matter of seconds. Good taste and intelligence also can act as a brake on the rest of an actor's equipment. But only if they are excessively relied on. You despise good taste, I know. Would you boast that you had bad taste?'

'I don't know whether it's good or bad but it's my own, it's me, and that's what I want to express.'

'That you can't help expressing, to some extent, but I am not trying to flatter you if I say that there is a lot more to you than you can possibly yet imagine at your age and probably what you fancy is *you* may appear very – you must forgive the word – adolescent when you are twice your present age . . .'

'I don't care what I feel about myself when I am twice my age! It is what I feel now that matters!'

'You are, I suppose, not old enough to have followed any actor's career for very long, but when you have done so you will notice that generally speaking one of two things happens with his 'personality.' Either it becomes coarser or it becomes finer. You say that it is what you are now that interests you, and in a sense you are right for what you are now is what you will always be. What you make of such attributes as you have is, in terms of expression, that is, of acting, a matter of technique. It is through technique that you will be able to project whatever it is that you wish to project and it is through technique that you will discover that there are a whole lot of other facets to your personality which are equally interesting and equally true to yourself.

I know that the word technique gives you slight feelings of nausea but, believe me, it is a word for something that exists, which is useful and which after a time becomes essential to the actor.'

Another pause.

'I think I'll go to the audition tomorrow morning.'

'I know you will go. Not, my dear friend, because of what I've said, but because, like most of us, you need a job. Forgive me for having perhaps laboured my point. Old actors, however, are not the only class of people who like to air the bees in their bonnets rather more than their friends would like. Besides, if one feels that there is anything of value in one's obsessions, it follows that one has to risk boring people in order to make sure that they shall understand. Good luck at the audition!'

The young man smiles. '*Merde!*'

'That's only a different way of putting the same thought.'

TO BE ME

OR NOT TO BE ME

NOTES ON 'THE METHOD'

IT SEEMS that the Method is catching on in England. It is headline news. Visiting American stars of the more recent vintages are interviewed on the subject and there is an undeniable, if indefinable, aura about them – or is it that their interviewers decline to define it, preferring to think that although this recent aspect of the actor's craft may be called the Method, discussion of it must still remain a *mystique*? Certainly the terminology is employed in England wildly. An 'armpit actor' has here been used to describe an old-fashioned actor, presumably because such actors are supposed to raise their arms to heaven, whereas what is meant is an actor who scratches his armpits: 'a torn T-shirt actor.' A leading ballet critic, deploring the allegedly unsatisfactory *mime* of our male ballet dancers, hazarded that a course of 'methodist' acting might be a help to them. Even *The Times* carried a headline a few months ago: *Schooling English Actors in the Method*. I am not suggesting that *The Times* does not frequently carry interesting articles on more or less up-to-date artistic tendencies; what mildly astonished me was to see 'The Method' referred to without quotes: the Method. Just like that. A significant accolade, I could not help thinking.

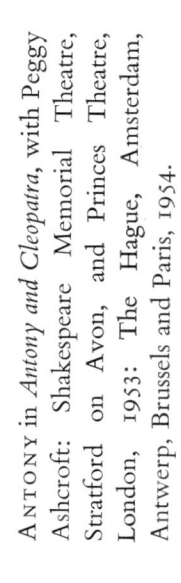

ANTONY in *Antony and Cleopatra*, with Peggy Ashcroft: Shakespeare Memorial Theatre, Stratford on Avon, and Princes Theatre, London, 1953: The Hague, Amsterdam, Antwerp, Brussels and Paris, 1954.

SHYLOCK in *The Merchant of Venice*, with Morris Carnovsky: Midnight Matinee for Helen Hayes's jubilee, Waldorf-Astoria, New York, 1955.

THE COLONEL in *Jacobowsky and the Colonel*, with Diana Gould and Esmé Percy: Piccadilly Theatre, 1945.

PHILIP LESTER in *A Touch of the Sun*, with Diana Wynyard and Vanessa Redgrave: Saville Theatre, 1958.

It is not surprising that the Method should gain some kind of foothold here sooner or later; though perhaps we should stress, here being England, later. Anyway, it's catching on now and in a big way. The only question is: whose Method? For, as *The Times* correspondent pointed out, with, as far as he went, accuracy and only the smallest discernible ambivalence, there are more than one.

There are indeed. There is of course the fountainhead: the Stanislavski method, which is chiefly concerned with the actor's work on himself. His book *An Actor Prepares* was first available in England about twenty years ago. It would not be fair to say that it has had little or no influence, for it has given inspiration, an intermittent flash like a lighthouse in a fog, to a great number of students and to some of our actors, but its influence has been surprisingly small in terms of making English actors want to go and do likewise. If it has been a lighthouse, it has – to continue the nautical metaphor – provided no fix. But then the Stanislavski system never pretended to be anything but what has been called 'a conscious codification' of what many good actors do instinctively without questioning why. It would surprise me to learn that Dame Peggy Ashcroft, or Miss Brenda de Banzie, for instance, keep a copy of Stanislavski's work near their pillows; but they and numbers of other actors and actresses have been, whether they are conscious of it or not, or whether they like it or not, Stanislavski-ites for years.

This may seem obvious. What is often forgotten is that Stanislavski did not intend his system to be used consciously and intellectually except when the actor, while in process of creating a performance, senses some break in its continuity. He then instinctively will stop and try to find out what has gone wrong. This may take time, and if the secret does not disclose itself from a re-examination of part of the scene or all of it, it may be necessary to re-examine the structure of the rôle and its relation to the play. It may even be necessary to re-examine the play. This is often the moment when lines or scenes are cut, rewritten or added. It is the moment when Gilbert Miller thinks that what the play needs is a different chandelier in Act ii.

For all these adjustments except the last the old system can be invaluable in that it provides a sort of catechism. Its technical terms – its 'units' and 'objectives' and 'super-objectives' – sound a little cold and arthritic in the English translation, but a catechism is after all a 'solemn interrogation' and Stanislavski's is a very thorough one.

Another point which is forgotten because of the myopic way in which the system is for the most part used is that Stanislavski, at any rate in his later years, expressly instructed his actors to be prepared to *act* and to discover the 'truth' of their acting through the doing of it. They were not taught to insist that they must 'feel' everything before they did it.

This last is where the latest manifestation of the Method, the one from the Actors' Studio in New York, is notoriously heretical and which, together with several other distortions of Stanislavski's precepts – not all inviolable by any means – is one of the causes of the widespread criticism of the Actors' Studio in New York. This queasiness with what is undeniably a remarkable and potent, but I think limited, influence seems not yet to be guessed at in London.

If at this point I mention that I have for years been 'on the record' as a champion of the New York Actors' Studio, I hope it will not seem that I am protesting too much. For in truth I have always been one of its more half-hearted champions. When I wrote of it a few years ago I was mourning the passing of the

London Theatre Studio, cut off by the war; and of the Old Vic School, closed because the Governors of the Old Vic had to choose between closing that or possibly having to close the Old Vic itself for lack of funds. The cost of preserving the Old Vic School and the Young Vic, and of continuing the teaching in England of Michel St. Denis, who had been offered the Comédie Française at the end of the war but who chose to remain in London with his colleagues of the London Theatre Studio, among whom were Mr. Glen Byam Shaw and Mr. George Devine, was – so St. Denis informed me at that time – a mere three to four thousand pounds a year, or the cost of presenting a 'one-set,' 'straight' play. These schools did an incalculable amount of good work, as the talents of many of our best young actors, directors and designers still prove. They were the most thorough theatre schools outside Russia; thorough and imaginative. Of course I am only going on what I have been told or have read about Russia, and it is another guess, a wishful one perhaps, when I say that some of our older established English Schools such as the R.A.D.A. are now less conventional, less unreluctantly débutantish than they were. But in 1953 it did not look like it, and I expressed the wish that, bereft of anything like the London Theatre Studio, we had here something like the New York Actors' Studio, where trained actors could take, from time to time, a 'refresher course.'

Well, now we have it. The young directors of the London Studio, according to the report in *The Times* of August 29th, and other sources, are at pains to point out that there are several differences between the handling of their classes and Mr. Lee Strasberg's method in New York:

'A typical meeting is attended by about 20 members; an arbitrator... invites groups of two or three to take the floor and submit some prepared work to general scrutiny. Scenes are rarely improvised ("it encourages slickness") ...'

I do not understand what is meant by improvisation encouraging slickness. The capacity to improvise is part of the stock-in-trade of the actor's craft. Any actor who is frightened of it must be frightened only by the word itself or by his fear of being cut off from his main source of supply: the author's text. Any actor, even the most timid, is improvising at the very first day of rehearsal and some of these first-day improvisations become set. They may sometimes deteriorate, but they are often true. The actor may improvise – on a given theme, of course – long after the first night. New inflexions, new business can be invented or refined or altered, within the framework of the production, long after the fiftieth performance. No two performances are identical, just as no interpretation or production can ever truly be said to be 'definitive.' A production or a painting can be the last and best of a line, but it cannot be definitive until the line is over the boundary, and the boundaries of art, especially interpretative art, are fluid, constantly changing, and the demarcations are all but imperceptible. I suggest that Irving's interpretation of *The Bells* may be one of the few examples of the 'definitive' in theatrical art.

'Reading from script is banned' says the same report. All right. 'Exercises remote from human experience (imitating a cash register for instance) have been allowed to remain in New York.' Sensible, and quite suitable. 'So has autocratic discipline,' the report continues; 'the arbitrator acts merely as a chairman.'

Pause here (I think to myself) and wonder whether this is an implied criticism of Mr. Strasberg or perhaps the modesty of the young directors-chairmen-arbitrators of the London branch. Both? One? Or neither? But in any case, is it a good thing?

Even the most democratic chairmen must retain something of autocratic discipline, or they would cease to discharge their function. Still, we may give them the benefit of the doubt about this and assume that it is their modesty, combined perhaps with youth and inexperience.

But having granted that, we may well be taken aback by what *The Times* describes as their 'declared intention to undermine the existing styles of acting in the English theatre.'

Not standards, we note, not 'some existing styles,' but styles.

Well, first of all, it is extremely difficult to lay a finger on what is meant by styles in acting, for when you come to analyse them you find that acting styles are actors' styles, invented and imposed, empirically, by a few actors in their time and grafted from one generation to another. It is not difficult to trace a history of English styles in acting Shakespeare, for instance, but it cannot be done without mentioning, apart from such reformers as Granville-Barker and William Poel, the names of actors and actresses. Our 'style' of acting Restoration drama narrows itself to comparatively few players, but many of them still living, for Restoration drama was only restored to us within living memory, thanks largely to the now defunct Phœnix Society. At the comedy of Humours our race of eccentrics has always excelled, and we are adept at amusing ourselves (and others when we perform it) with a kind of entertainment in which the players, like some water insects, seem to be supported only by surface-tension.

Why should anyone want to 'undermine' these things, such as they are and not without honour? It would be easy here to make a list of names, writers and players, plays, past and present, adding: 'Our own, and not such poor things neither.' Would it not be pertinent to inquire what styles the London Actors' Studio from New York intends to mould to replace them?

Mr. Ben Gazzara, interviewed by Miss Dilys Powell, who asked him what would the Method do for Shakespearean acting, replied 'with a smile' that it would slow it up. I like him for that, but he should have added 'to a standstill.' How, I would like to know, would the Method help an actress to play Millament, where the character as well as the wit is almost entirely contained in the phrasing? Wondrous as it would be to have a film record of Edith Evans' performance in that rôle, nine-tenths of it is conveyed and the essence captured in the recordings she has made. If we need some propping-up (not undermining) in our Restoration style, which we do, for it is more manner than style with most of us, we should turn to the Brecht actors rather than the Actors' Studio. When Miss Ruth Gordon dazzled London in *The Country Wife* at the Old Vic over twenty years ago she possessed the character completely, while at the same time standing so well outside it that she seemed to be sitting in the audience's lap. Indeed Miss Gordon, though she could break our hearts with her realistic Mattie in *Ethan Frome*, might well have been one of Brecht's favourite actresses.

It would be fitter, perhaps, and a shade more dignified, to leave the 'declared intentions' of the London Actors' Studio to echo briefly in an insular silence. To judge from the columns of *The Times*, no one here seems perturbed, except Mr. Giles Playfair, and he writes from Massachusetts. But I have spent the better part of the last two theatrical seasons in New York and I think the threat deserves a little more attention than a huffy, British aloofness. One cannot be sure, even in *The Times* (alas!) that the phrase 'undermine the existing styles' is verbatim, but it has the typical nihilistic ring.

British acting in New York has been popular with the public there for many years. (Too many, some American actors think.) And this is not surprising, in view of the comparatively short history of the American theatre; for it is only in the last three decades or less that the Americans have found an acting style of their own, based on plays of American life. A very excellent style it is, full of the vitality and violence, the diversity, the warmth and richness as well as the starkness of their civilisation. But not all plays can be indigenous. It is right that Broadway should also want to see other playwrights: Giraudoux and Anouilh (though these two have so far chalked up only three successes there between them) and Rattigan (two successes) and other contemporary foreign playwrights. They want to see the Old Vic, the Comédie Française. They are hospitable to Jean-Louis Barrault, the Habima Players and a host of others, not to mention singers and dancers. The lack of theatres in New York is as desperate as in London. The economics more so, for the public can be persuaded to pay only scant attention to anything but the smart hits. It has been educated or bullied to do so. The salaries in the two countries are so different that, whereas it is tempting for an English actor to go to New York with a commensurate guarantee, an American actor will only come here to act for prestige, or fun, or some other not necessarily commercial reason.

It follows that there is, in certain quarters, a marked resentment of English actors in New York, just as there is, in certain professional quarters, a resentment of visiting Americans here. It would be difficult to say which side comes out of this to the better credit, if any. We think we do; they think they do. The warmth and size of the welcome given in New York to English actors make it unfitting for me to discuss the current chauvinism to be found there occasionally, beyond remarking that it is not confined to dear Helen Hayes' recent outburst – regrettable and much regretted by her. But I think it has to be mentioned. And some of the blame must be laid at the door of the Actors' Studio, many of whose members wear their membership with the same lack of grace that they would detest in anyone sporting 'the old school tie.'

I think never before, in the history of either country, has anyone declared his intention of changing, or undermining, the other's style of doing anything. (Except, of course, in Big Business.) It is a bold claim, but is it a futile one? There would be many in New York who would say it is by no means impotent and point with despair to what has happened in their own theatre where, around a small group of brilliant and talented actors, has arisen a much larger group of hangers-on who possess little of their talent. There is a cult of the inarticulate, the violent and the selfish.

Individually most of them are engaging to meet. There is a certain amount of cultivated rudeness, designed to draw attention, but one remembers that pleasant manners and a neat appearance have at no time or place been considered the hallmarks of genius. They are tremendous workers, for an actor has to work hard in a theatre where over ninety-two per cent are unemployed. The worst that is said of them individually is the phrase which seems to have been coined for them: 'crazy mixed-up kids!'

It is when you come to work with them that you come up against an obstinacy which is like a brick wall covered with foam mattress. Many of them will go to dancing classes (to get into musicals), take singing lessons (for the same reason) as well as acting classes. But mention the word 'technique,' mention the 'voice' as apart from a voice that will get you a job in a musical, mention almost any of the accepted terms if you dare. All that they want to know about is feeling. By this they mean *their* feeling, and very subjective and 'off-beat' that feeling can be. In the New York theatre world there is a famous story which when it was new was thought funny, of two Studio actors waiting for their entrance. One of them kept doubling in agony. His companion asked him what was wrong. He groaned 'I've got a belly ache.' 'Fine!' was the reply, 'USE IT!'

It is justly levelled against English actors that they have too much facility, and a very strong case could be brought against what an English critic has called the 'effortless, impactless' style of some of our 'surface-tension' actors when they find themselves out of their depth in the wrong kind of play. In New York, to give a good first reading is to lay oneself open to being thought a 'radio actor.' To avoid this grave charge, a great deal of artificial fumbling and inarticulacy, punctuated by long pauses, can go on. In one of the two plays that I have directed in New York, I cast a youngish actor in the small part of a servant, Matvei in Turgenev's *A Month in the Country*. I was at pains to say that I did not expect a finished conception of any part at the first reading but that I would be by no means displeased if any actor gave a coherent interpretation. A moderate injunction, one might think, to give in a city where such a director as Mr. Garson Kanin instructed the cast of *The Diary of Anne Frank*, so it is said, to learn their words before the first rehearsal. Matvei is a small part; unusually direct and simple as parts in Russian plays go. But, as it was a small part, I let go by for three days an extraordinary mixture of hesitant fumbling in which scarcely a sentence of the deliberately simple phrases was intact. On the fourth day (a fateful one in New York because unless the actor has a run-of-the-play contract he can then be discharged if thought to be unsatisfactory) I reminded him firstly that country people, when expressing simple thoughts, are usually extremely direct and, secondly, that in a play full of vacillating characters who cannot make up their minds about what they want or why they want it, a modest, straightforward, plain-spoken man was provided by the author as a point of balance. I added that the simplicity of the character was not only true to type but might conceivably prove theatrically effective. I advised him then on the fateful fourth day to speak the lines quite simply in a loud clear voice and to see what happened. What happened was sufficiently plausible for me to say 'You see? That's more or less it!' At the end of that rehearsal he came up to me and asked, not without a twinkle, 'I guess this is one of these occasions when the actor has to sink his ego to the production?' I replied disingenuously, 'Don't you always do that?'

Matvei was played on the first night as written and directed; or more or less so, for the actor could not or would not persuade himself that something more could not be done with it. It is a current phrase in the New York Actors' Studio that there is 'no such thing as a small part; there are only small actors.' When I last saw the production before leaving New York, I saw as the chief servant of this Russian household of 1840, most of whom spoke French and whose sense was in inverse ratio to their sensibility, a poor cretin who crept into the elegant drawing-room, bowed and scraped in abject terror, and whose simplest words were hard to apprehend. I half expected that on one of his exits he would go off humming the Volga Boat Song.

Mr. Burl Ives, in his unforgettable performance as 'Big Daddy' in *Cat on a Hot Tin Roof*, became disturbed, he told me, one night during one of his longer speeches, by the sound of a spoon tinkling in a cocktail mixer somewhere upstage of him. He later asked the actor – one of several who played his son during the long run of the play – why the hell he had to mix himself *another* cocktail at that point. Didn't the character (an alcoholic) mix enough cocktails as it was. The young man replied that he was not mixing another cocktail, just tinkling. 'What for?' He got the stock Studio answer: 'Just making a life for myself on the stage.'

Such betrayals of the author's word, which should be the actor's bond, are not the sole property of the Actors' Studio nor of New York. You will find them elsewhere, if you look for them. But the extraordinary self-righteous justification of them is, I think, more noticeable in New York, where the discipline, when it is bad, is somewhat worse than the worst in England. You could, if you wished, defend them by saying that the treachery is deliberate and therefore preferable to the *laissez-faire*, happy-go-lucky, lax standards which here and there obtain in the English theatre. You could point to half a hundred plays, from *Golden Boy* to *A View from the Bridge* where team work and fidelity to the text have gone handsomely hand in hand. I would agree. I would agree that Julie Harris is a fine actress and Marlon Brando a remarkable actor. I would believe them willingly if they told me that they owe as much to the Actors' Studio as the Actors' Studio owes to them; but the fact remains that they would have been remarkable whatever studio or school of acting they had attended.

What the Actors' Studio aims to achieve is not, immediately, results. Its aim is to allow the actor, in Stanislavski's phrase, 'to work with himself.' That is an excellent idea. It is also excellent that the Studio should be exclusive, selecting its students by a rigorous standard. It is remarkable and enviable that such opportunity as it gives should be given without fees or dues. Much as I distrust the idea that actors should be encouraged in free and frank criticism of each other's experiments I cannot help admiring the courage of it. (The late James Dean is reported to have been unable to attend class for several weeks after his initiation.) But I also cannot help remembering that this ruthless and often exhibitionist kind of criticism is said to have been one of the causes of the disruption of the American Group Theatre in the thirties. 'At times, there was an invisible silent slaughter going on among the Group actors,' says Mr. Harold Clurman, one of their leading spirits and their historian, in his brilliant book *The Fervent Years*, ' . . . At night I was wakened by solicitous telephone calls from some actor who couldn't sleep because of another actor's performance and by day I received friendly letters from fellow workers advising me on how I might overcome the defects in my latest productions, listing them with remarkable patience.'

The Group was, without doubt, the most remarkable phenomenon of the modern American theatre, creating a style of its own, an ensemble which has seldom if ever been surpassed, and a number of very remarkable actors and directors, and giving scope to some playwrights. I am sure that Mr. Lee Strasberg, who was one of its leaders, would not claim that the Actors' Studio has yet equalled these achievements. He would almost certainly remark that these things are not what the Actors' Studio is for. 'The work at the Studio does not aim at results.' Nevertheless, some plays have emerged from the Studio, notably *A Hatful of Rain* and *End as a Man* (both now filmed). I wonder what Mr. Strasberg thinks of these, to my mind, crude melodramas, so eccentrically, so egocentrically, performed. I am not alone in thinking that the New York production of the former was a trunkful of tricks and anyone who has seen the film of the latter and can praise it for its ensemble playing had better stick to Mr. Emlyn Williams as Dickens.

Mr. Lee Strasberg possesses enormous theatrical erudition and evidently, when on the job, a remarkable personality. Like many born teachers he is not notably a doer. He is a catalyst. What he releases in a genuine and remarkable talent is genuine and better than remarkable. What happens to the less gifted is sometimes fortunate, often factitious. The third-rate remain, in the end, third-rate. That, I suppose, is the pattern of all teaching. The silk purse and the sow's ear, the brick and the straw remain constants.

Yet one of Mr. Strasberg's favourite dicta is that if the first-rate would work with the persistency of genius it might seem to equal genius, and that with the same ratio of application the fifth can elevate itself to the first-grade. It is a humdrum-sounding dictum but it has the lustre of a truth. Why then does it seldom seem to be fulfilled among the student-practitioners of the Actors' Studio? For the same reason—it would be easy and obvious to say—that most geese and ugly-ducklings cannot turn into swans. However hard they try, it sooner or later becomes evident to them that it is not of what is in their stars but of what is not in themselves.

The chance, the hope-around-the-corner, the lottery aspects of life light up the world of the theatre with the spasmodic brilliance of the latest *marquee* sign. The frontier of the theatre is, of all the arts, the easiest to cross. There are no guards to turn you back; no one drives any one else out of the enchanted forest, except a few skirmishers who, having lost their way early, turn angrily on those at their heels and shout about 'restricted entry.'

The actors at the Actors' Studio, whose work, as I have said, is not for immediate results, are encouraged to turn ever inwards onto their own personal problems. The 'psycho-technique' of Stanislavski, by which he tried to make the 'sub-conscious function naturally' through the 'grammar' of playing which he attempted to codify, is all too frequently abandoned and free-play is given to the subjective, the personal and the odd. No matter how irrelevant to the scene being played, the actor's quirks and quiddities are explored to see if they make dramatic material suitable for him.

For Mr. Strasberg is a 'deviationist' from the original 'Method' especially where 'emotive memory' is concerned.

'Do you think' Stanislavski asks his (imaginary) student 'that it would be wise for an actor to give himself up to such spontaneous emotions as that?' 'Time is a splendid filter' he has previously remarked 'for our remembered feelings – besides it is a great artist. It not only purifies, it transmutes even painfully realistic memories into poetry.' The student asks if such spontaneous emotions are never desirable. The teacher replies that on the contrary they are most desirable, but that these direct, powerful and vivid emotions do not make their appearance on the stage in the way we think. They flash, but they do not last. They are often irrelevant to the matter in hand.

'The unfortunate thing about them is that we cannot control them, they control us. Therefore we have no choice but to leave it to nature and say: "If they will come, let them come!" We only hope that they will work with the part and not at cross purposes to it.'

We should not laugh at the earnest endeavour to act an inanimate object, such as a typewriter, or the other exercises in sense-and-emotion-memory. I even wish, in a perverse kind of way, that I had seen the actor who gave an exercise as Richard II in prison based on his fear of rats. We should not laugh, for the reason that any experiment, if sincerely conducted, may conceivably find a grain of a grain of truth among the chaff. The danger is that what is seized on and preserved, in this passionate quest for originality, is not the essential but the decorative, or even the waste product.

The essence of a work of art is found in its form, content or style. This is not an age of style. It is an age where texture matters more than form. The texture, taste, touch, the tang of a thing mean more, or rather sell better, than a sense of style. 'Style' has become a dirty word, like 'sincerity.'

But style, like sincerity, has not lost its head nor its sense of direction. Symmetry mysteriously remains symmetry, and symmetry and style have a mathematical or logical cohesion which texture, tang and touch can never have. Style courts inevitability. The other things rush to embrace the unexpected and achieve only ornament.

I can pay Mr. Strasberg no greater compliment than to say that I wish him the same kind of brilliantly talented pupils which he, and another iconoclastic genius, Mr. Gordon Craig, deserve. But by the nature of things there will be very few of them. I hope that their talents are not only brilliant but have as much of the indestructible as it is possible for talent short of genius to possess. They may find what it is that the Actors' Studio is seeking and it may be something more elevating and less obscurantist than is now visible. Yes, and more truthful.

To the less indestructible I can only recommend a strict and arduous, however pedestrian, course in what is already known about acting.

The first thing that is known is that you must be prepared to get up and do it. If you can't do that because you know you will make mistakes, you had better pack up. To use an adage so hoary that it is almost new: it is like trying to milk a he-goat with a sieve.

Cézanne, in a letter to Roger Marx, says: 'To my mind, one should not substitute oneself for the past, one has merely to add a new link.' One supposes that the Actors' Studio actress who last summer essayed her first Juliet (in New York's Central Park) has heard of the French impressionists, for she has been reported to exclaim: 'I see the part in pastels and they want me to play it in oils!' She was gently and justly rebuked by someone who said: 'But it's written in oils!' Anyway, she got up and did it and, from what I have read, with some success.

SHAKESPEARE AND

THE ACTORS

MY ACQUAINTANCE with the acting of Shakespeare's plays began in Stratford, here in the old theatre of which this Conference Hall is now the shell. Inconceivable to me, almost, that in this horseshoe of a wall I saw *Richard III*, *Macbeth*, and also, to give them their 'professional' names, *Antony*, *The Dream*, *The Wives*, *Merchant* and, as if for good measure, *School*. Yet most memorable were the days in my summer holidays when I was allowed to walk-on and throw rose petals at the coronation of the young King Henry the Fifth. Was there 'no Equity stirring?' And were those paper petals fire-proofed, one now wonders? However, it was not after a performance of *Henry IV Part II*, that the old theatre was, so mercifully, gutted. Mercifully? How can one be so ungrateful to a theatre which relieved at least this one child of ever having to say 'Shakespeare was killed for me at school?' I loved Shakespeare at school. But mainly, I think, because I had already seen some of his plays acted here, where thirty years ago my mother was acting in the Memorial Theatre Company. Afterwards, from a brief acquaintance as a somewhat flat-chested public-school Lady Macbeth when the lines

> I would, while it was smyling in my Face,
> Have pluckt my Nipple from his Bonelesse Gummes

were bowdlerised to

> Have plucked my breast from out his boneless gums

I progressed to 'Cambridge Shakespeare,' acted by what was for some strange, though some would now have us think prophetic, reason the Marlowe Society. Here I played a few parts. Now, I am told, each undergraduate in his time plays many. I envy him. I played as many as I could, disregarding the warnings of my tutors.

Even in those days (the late 1920's), there were rumours abroad in the great world that the intelligentsia held the Marlowe Society in high esteem. Please do not mistake me. I had and have what I hope is a proper regard for the intelligentsia. As Lady Bracknell might have said:

'Never speak disrespectfully of Bloomsbury, Algy; only those who can't get into it do that.'

But I noticed even then a strong tendency in some quarters, mainly academic and literary, and one which I do not think has much decreased, to assume that the performances given by the Shakespearean amateurs such as were given by the Marlowe Society, or the O.U.D.S. or by well-taught schoolboys, were altogether preferable to those given by professional actors. Preferable, apparently, by the highest if not all standards. I have never, so far as I remember, seen a performance by the O.U.D.S., but I will take full responsibility, as a former member of the Marlowe Society who acted in several plays and who has witnessed others, to say that the standard of verse-speaking (its chief pride) was distinctly below that which is nowadays attained in the better professional productions. It is about time this should be said. It was asserted for long that professional Shakespearean productions paid scant attention to Shakespeare's words and Shakespeare's wishes. The charge had some truth in it. But how much? And is the standard of the Marlowe Society in reality a standard at all, except for those for whom it is intended? A standard, certainly, but a very specialised, small standard.

Sir Desmond MacCarthy, reviewing a book on Elizabethan acting, referred to the difference – a difference of which he said he had been aware all his life – 'between those who love the theatre and those who much prefer "literary experience".' All of us are, I assume, aware of this difference and Shakespeare of all authors makes us sense it most keenly. Those who 'love the theatre' also tend to love the actor and regard even the greatest parts not merely as a challenge to the actor but as set pieces which the actor may paint with his own personality and virtuosity more or less as he will. Even in music, the purest of the arts, we will prefer to hear one musician in Mozart, another in Beethoven, a third in Chopin. The highest praise we can bestow on any musician is to imply that his style in Mozart or Beethoven comes nearest to what we imagine Mozart or Beethoven to require. The highest praise we can give to a Shakespearean actor is to say that his performance persuaded us that this is the Dane that Shakespeare drew. It is a rare accolade. On the other hand, those who prefer 'literary experience' tend to regard the actor with some suspicion, as a vulgariser, 'an upstart crow, beautified with our Shakespeare's feathers.' There is much truth in the belief that in the theatre, as in the study, the poet's words are all that count but it is not, as Sir Desmond remarked, the whole truth. 'Vitally important as the poet's words are – or for that matter, his ideas – in the theatre something else also counts: namely the actor's power to make us feel as if he really was the man he impersonates. It is not everything or 'all' that we should exclaim 'How perfectly he spoke that speech! With what nicety of intonation he marked its changing meanings!' The summit of the actor's art is also to make us forget that he is an actor; only then do we share intimately the experiences of his character's creator.'

This summit of the actor's art may or may not be, as Sir Desmond said, accompanied by intelligence. There have been good actors who were deficient in taste as well as brains. But perhaps it is not claiming too much for our present English theatre if one suggests that despite various 'experiments,' certain productions noted more for their power to shock than to convince, Shakespearean production and acting in England today is certainly truer to the text, closer not only to the poet's words but to their meaning than in any of the three centuries which divide us from Shakespeare's lifetime. Of course when we think of Davenant's version of *Macbeth* in the seventeenth century, with that curious scene between Lady Macbeth and Lady Macduff, or of Nahum Tate and Colley Cibber, or of Garrick's happy ending to *King Lear*, we may not think that this is a very large claim. At the same time, your minds may challenge the claim with memories of certain 'stunt' productions; a black and white *Twelfth Night* (very innocent, this), various modern dress *Hamlets*, an aluminium *Macbeth*, a production of *As You Like It* with Rosalind as Ganymede dressed as a boy scout and Celia as a girl guide, a *Henry VIII* with a royal family dressed as a pack of cards – all these may make you think the claim that today's productions are nearer to Shakespeare an absurdly bold one. But even some of those deliberately over-daring, 'shocking' productions have, I think, had their value and will, I hope, from time to time be followed by others, for they have frequently given a jolt to accepted ideas of both character and style and though they may not have replaced the ideas which they have shaken with anything notably more durable, one or two scenes, a speech, a minor character, some way of staging those almost impossible scenes which every producer of Shakespeare is confronted with have had their effect on our general consciousness of Shakespearean production; and, just as the designs of Gordon Craig, so seldom put into practice in the theatre, nevertheless revolutionised to some extent our ideas of Shakespearean décor, so these experiments, however costly they seemed at the time, have in some cases been of considerable value.

The history of the theatre – like the history of the world – is chiefly notable for the slowness with which general ideas change. There are of course many reasons for this, in the theatre as in life, many of them economic. All modern producers have been aware, for some decades past, of the limitations of the Picture Frame Stage. Yet we are in most cases powerless to change it. I like to think that the policy of our governments, who will not allow us permits to rebuild our bombed theatres, may prove a blessing in disguise, like the Fire of London, and that by the time we do get permits our revolt against the picture frame will have grown – as it will grow – so strong that the new theatres will be truly *new* theatres.

But in talking of Shakespearean production I am putting the cart before the horse, for I am supposed to speak on Shakespeare and the actors. 'Why,' one is frequently asked, 'are there so many revivals of Shakespeare in London and elsewhere?' 'Why do you not do more new plays? Is it true that there are so few new plays that are worthwhile?' As for the last question, I think the ratio of worthwhile new plays is not remarkably low nor so remarkably high, but what is very notable from the actor's point of view is that in the last half-century, since the advent of

Shaw, Chekov and other playwrights who have most notably influenced the art of theatre writing, there is a conspicuous absence of really great parts. The emphasis, in production as well as in playwriting, has been on *team playing*, on the *ensemble*; a healthy emphasis no doubt, insofar as only with team playing can one ever hope to see the perfect production of any play, Shakespearean or otherwise, where the whole thing – acting, production, setting – makes a perfect synthesis. But this scarcity of great parts in worthwhile plays compels the truly 'aspiring actor' to turn to Shakespeare. There he can hope to find, among the many great parts that Shakespeare wrote, several, or at least a few, which he feels he has a right to tackle and which challenge him and stretch him to breaking point and sometimes beyond it, and it is not very difficult to imagine that once an actor has played his Hamlet, his Richard II, his Lear, his Benedick, the worthwhile parts in worthwhile modern plays on the whole do not seem to challenge him or to test his full powers. The actor deals most forcefully when he deals in passions, in tears and terror – a thing that Ibsen understood – or in gargantuan Falstaffian humours – a thing that Sean O'Casey and the late James Bridie have understood. And in the scarcity of such parts the actor turns where for three centuries, in all languages, he has turned; and where the public, numbed by the anaesthetic of a peaceful labour revolution or racked by the pangs of world revolution, also turns: to Shakespeare.

What does an actor do when he first decides to play or is offered one of these great Shakespearean parts? Sometimes, indeed frequently, it is a part about which he has been thinking, sometimes vividly, sometimes confusedly, for a number of years. Very often his approach may to some extent be governed by some facet of the character which, in his own mind, he has perceived to be in that character but has never seen performed to his satisfaction. I know, for instance, that a great deal of my conception of Hamlet was coloured by what I thought was the misconception, so heavily stressed in the film of *Hamlet*, that this was the tragedy of 'a man who could not make up his mind.' For to me it is very clear that Hamlet could make up his mind as well as anybody else, given those terrible circumstances, would be able to do. In the same way, I have always so strongly rejected the suggestion that Hamlet was in any way a victim of what we so lightly call an Oedipus complex that I used every possible opportunity to express Hamlet's love for his father. To take another example with which I am intimately acquainted, it seems to me that when you study Richard II there is no getting round the fact that Richard behaves like a petty tyrant at the beginning of the play, and the fact that Shakespeare has given Richard no early scene to show us any of the sweetness of Richard's character can in no way excuse the actor for glossing over Richard's cruelty and spite towards the dying Gaunt, his envy and resentment of the man he has banished, his sexual inversion nor his flippancy and disregard towards the Queen. In being anxious to be honest about all these things in Richard's character at the beginning I, especially at the early performances, over-stressed these matters out of an unconscious fear that no one would see the point. So much for some preconceived ideas which may well colour a whole performance.

While I am talking of testing and breaking as well as making, something occurs to me that I have felt very forcibly in the last year or two: that no actor can really master one of these great rôles at a first performance. But there are many other pre-conceived, or rather, second-hand or third-hand ideas which have to be sorted out, preferably before rehearsals start. Let me take a very well-known model. Of all the Shakespearean parts, Hamlet has suffered the most from the accretion of three centuries and of many countries. We are aware of Hamlet theories which we may never have read, of whose origin we are ignorant. All actors, it is said, want to play Hamlet. Listening to my friends and reading here and there, I do not think, indeed, that there is anyone, actor or spectator, who does not think, with Coleridge, that 'I have a smack of Hamlet myself, if I may say so.' At some time or another all actors have seen Hamlet played, one supposes. In my own case I was enormously impressed by John Gielgud's first Hamlet, played at the Old Vic over twenty years ago. This performance I saw several times and when I first performed the part as an amateur in 1932 my memory of Gielgud was so strong that I must have seemed like Gielgud's understudy. Since I was determined to play the part professionally one day I obliged myself – and this was no easy thing to do – not to see any of Gielgud's later interpretations. In the matter of Richard II, again, I have been tremendously influenced by my vivid memories of Gielgud in the part, especially in the scenes when I was on the stage with him playing Bolingbroke. That is some thirteen or fourteen years ago but Ivor Brown was quite right to detect that on the first night this season I had still traces of Gielgud's intonations. Gradually, during the run of *Richard II* this year, as my own characterisation has grown I have found that more and more of these what might be called Gielgudisms have disappeared. There are others, however, of which I am still aware and which I would not dream of altering. The phrasing and breathing of the speech at the Lists when Richard banishes Bolingbroke and Mowbray are something which Gielgud managed with such dazzling skill that I do not see how they could be better done, nor do I see

any reason to be too proud to imitate his technical framework of that cadenza which begins with
> Draw neere and list
> What with our councell we have done...
> (Act i, scene 3)

This is a point that one could develop to greater length. During the last forty years we have become increasingly distrustful of the traditional in acting; and rightly so, for often the traditional in acting becomes warped and hollow and insincere, preserving a decorative shell with no life in it. Our emphasis nowadays in acting is on originality and truth of feeling and it is quite unfashionable to suggest that one has copied or borrowed any part of another man's work. Nevertheless, a very great deal is copied and borrowed, sometimes unconsciously, sometimes not, not only in the matter of stage business where borrowing is as pardonable as it is prevalent, but in other matters. Nor can I see there is any harm in this. If, as someone has said, genius is a pool, it is one where all may be allowed to refresh themselves provided they do not make the water muddy.

But now for the mass of literary accretions. What is the actor to do about them? Would the ideal Hamlet be a young actor of genius who had never seen the play performed or read anything about its performances? I cannot think so. There are innumerable pitfalls and difficulties in the part of Hamlet, to many of which there are known guides. To disregard all of these would be like offering to explore rough country without a map. But which guide? And how many guides? In the German theatre under Reinhardt the producer was the sole guide and his conception and execution of a character were law. A German actor of that period would not have dreamed of disobeying. In spite of the growing importance of the producer in our theatre, that has never been the case with us, nor I think, is it ever likely to be and none of the leading actors of our theatre would embark on a leading rôle without some measure of agreement with the producer as to how the play was to be staged and interpreted.

Another preliminary agreement which has to be made either by the actor or the producer or both is at least some nodding acquaintance with present-day Shakespearean scholarship. As time goes on more and more books are written about Shakespeare and there is no sign that this flood will abate, especially in such a time as now when Shakespeare is more frequently played in our playhouses than he has ever been before. Professor Dover Wilson, lecturing here at Stratford a week or so ago, declared that the present time was probably the first time in which actors and scholars have really got together in the production of the plays. This does not mean, however, that the producer and the actor decide which scholar or scholars most suit their purposes and that they then invite them to sit in on the preliminary stages of rehearsals and supervise their plan of production. Though this might seem to be the ideal arrangement it is one which, for obvious reasons, would be very hard to put into practice, and personally I rather doubt whether it would work. Very few scholars, however much they may try, can envisage their theories being put into practice on the stage and I do not think it would be unfair to say that the major fault of Shakespearean criticism is that theories are deduced from the plays by lines being taken out of their context. This, of course, is also a fault of the actors and a great many actors tend to approach their parts with some strong personal feeling which has excited them from the reading of a few lines here and there. There is no end to what you *can* read into a Shakespearean part if you *try* – even into some of the smallest – and here again, as for the scholars, the golden rule should be: what is the context? When I am producing a play I always remind the actors to try to work out for themselves the answer to the question: why is their character in the play at all. Why did the author introduce such and such a character? This very simple step taken, it should be easy to perceive the character in its context. But believe it or not, it is extremely difficult to persuade a great many actors to do this. It is part of actors' make-up to imagine that the moment we step on to the stage the whole play more or less revolves round us, that all eyes are focussed on us. This is not altogether a bad thing, since the egotistic principle from which it springs very often gives force and life and vitality to a character that might otherwise sink into the background. But it is, of course, a very dangerous assumption.

Now, there is a most interesting historical example of a great actress giving an entirely personal reading of a part and with the greatest possible critical success. I mean Mrs. Siddons' Lady Macbeth. This, which is scarcely more than a theory of mine, is based on a most extraordinary piece of business which I first found recorded in the Furness Variorum edition of the play – an edition, by the way, which I always have by me during the preparation of a part and during rehearsals. From this and later editions I choose what readings seem to me theatrically clearest and most immediate to my general conception. If this shocks anyone, let me remind him that though there is certainly no definitive conception, nor ever will be, neither is there, nor ever will be, a definitive text.

I have digressed for a moment, but let me remind you of a theory held both by the editor of the *New Temple Shakespeare*, Mr. Roy Ridley, and also by Sir Lewis Casson, and which I first found suggested in the Variorum. It is this: that if Lady Macbeth shows signs of her ultimate breakdown before she leaves the stage at the end of the banquet scene (after which, you will remember, she disappears until the sleep-walking scene) she thereby minimises the pathos of the sleep-walking scene. Ridley argues, and rightly I think, that though there are lines into which you can read some hint of the on-coming breakdown, such as

> Nought's had, all's spent,
> Where our desire is got without content:
>
> (Act iii, scene 2)

there is no single line which can be taken to mean only that. The couplet I have just quoted can, after all, be perfectly well read in the character of the greedy ambitious woman who is never satisfied. Now on view in London at the Tate Gallery among the remarkable collection of theatrical pictures lent by the Garrick Club is a Zoffany showing Garrick and Mrs. Pritchard at the moment when Lady Macbeth says 'Give me the daggers.' And in the Garrick Club (I do not know whether it is on view at the Tate) is another picture of Mrs. Pritchard who, as you may remember, is best remembered for her performance of Lady Macbeth. It is a picture which I have stared at again and again, since it hangs opposite me at my favourite place in the Coffee Room at the Club. In both pictures we are shown a quite relentless face, marked by none of the traits of sensitivity and spirituality which you will find in any of the Siddons portraits. I am certain, from what I have read of Mrs. Pritchard's performance, that she would entirely have satisfied Ridley's conception and that it was her great successor who first introduced what we must call 'the modern Lady Macbeth,' the Lady Macbeth who begins to show signs of weakness when she realises that her husband is plotting Banquo's murder. For Mrs. Siddons, you will find in the records, did the most extraordinary and, to my mind, unforgivable, inartistic thing in the banquet scene: she pretended to see the ghost of Banquo and to overcome her fears. One can only suppose that her Macbeth on this occasion was a singularly ineffective actor, but even if he had been a great actor one could only suppose that Lady Macbeth would have secured all interest to herself by this extraordinary piece of business. And it is also clear, if you come to think of it, that two people frightened by a ghost on the stage are less effective than one.

One of the theatrical difficulties in *Hamlet*, by the way – and the difficulties on the stage are so much less difficult than the difficulties on paper – is that the protagonist is required to meet his father's ghost for the first time after several of the other characters have already met the ghost twice. We read much of how Garrick made a great play with his hands and how his start on seeing his father's ghost was widely copied and became almost a test piece of business for an actor. I was interested when I saw Alec Guinness's Hamlet recently to note that this, one of the most famous cruces in the play, was very beautifully solved by Hamlet doing precisely nothing, which, after the elaborate starts and gestures and striking with partisans by some of the other characters, was signally effective. Here again we have an instance of how 'tradition' can become 'convention'; and convention, in the theatre as elsewhere, can have a pulverising effect, and how one actor with imaginative genius can breathe life into a corpse. But to return to Lady Macbeth. It is well known, of course, that Mrs. Siddons made her name and was best remembered as the Dame of Cawdor. I do not suggest that her whole reading of the part was a wilful one. One is sure, from the descriptions of the murder scene, that she played it for all it is worth and as it is written. But I do suggest that she perhaps consciously wanted to do something that her great predecessor, Mrs. Pritchard, had not done, and that she deliberately played the scene before Banquo's murder and the banquet scene in such a way as to draw all attention to herself. In this she has been followed by nearly every actress ever since. Whether or not it robs the sleep-walking scene of some of its pathos it is difficult to say, for now-a-days even those who have never read *Macbeth* are anticipating the sleep-walking scene which is perhaps the most famous scene in the play. But I think Ridley is right, and that if we had never seen the play, the shock of the sleep-walking scene would be twice as effective if it had not been foreshadowed.

I may seem to be making a mountain of this small and almost forgotten instance, but it is a very typical example of how actors who want to put some personal conception on a character will quite flagrantly do so at the expense of the text. You may think this kind of interference with Shakespeare as impertinent as it is over-bold, but one of the formidable difficulties for the actor in attempting the great Shakespearean parts is that Shakespeare did not appear to take the trouble to dramatise, in the strict sense of the word, some important side of the character. We know, for instance, that Cleopatra was written for a boy and I think we can dismiss any wishful argument that in writing his great heroines Shakespeare foresaw the time when women would be allowed to act them. Though he may have done so, he certainly wrote them bearing the limitations of the boy-actors in mind, and for this reason there is no scene of love-making either in *Antony and Cleopatra* or in *Romeo and Juliet*, where the greatest love scene in dramatic literature keeps the lovers separated by a balcony's distance. We know this, or are reminded of it by scholars, but yet in every modern production of *Antony and Cleopatra*, if you read the notices you will find that the actress is somewhere or other blamed for not being sufficiently amorous, seductive or 'riggish.'

We arrive at the theatre with a romantic, vague but highly coloured picture of the ideal Cleopatra, who is, of course, not Shakespeare's Cleopatra. But this difficulty is not only confined to the women's parts, which, of course, were first created by boys; it also applies to some of the leading male characters of Shakespeare. For instance, Antony is described as 'noble' on no less than eight occasions. But, excepting for his generosity towards Enobarbus, and possibly in his death-scene, Antony is never *shown* to do one noble thing. If we accept his passion for Cleopatra we can only be dismayed by his acceptance of Octavia 'for his peace' and if we pity Octavia we must think less of him for his 'I will to Egypt,' spoken before he has even married her. Whoever play the parts of Antony and Cleopatra should look to it that they have a first-rate Enobarbus, for Enobarbus creates Antony's nobility and Cleopatra's fascination as much as the protagonists can hope to do.

But if Antony is a difficult part, how much more difficult, and notoriously so, is Macbeth. Here again, the audience arrives at the theatre with highly-coloured but vague expectations of this Scottish chieftain, this murderer; and here again we find that Macbeth is described as noble and valiant and during the whole play we see him do nothing that is either noble or valiant. This part is indeed what we may well call a teaser and it is notable that no actor has, as it were, claimed Macbeth as his own, although by all accounts, Garrick and Macready were very fine in it. And while I talk of the vague and colourful expectation which the audience brings to the theatre with them since all these great parts have enlarged themselves in people's imagination far beyond the bounds of the text, let me say that in my opinion a great deal must be laid at the door of the nineteenth century critics. It has been said that Bradley's *Hamlet* was 'better than Shakespeare's' and it is also true that people who have never read Bradley are to some extent Bradleians without knowing it. Bradley, like many of the nineteenth century critics, was a romantic, and romantics notoriously twist facts to suit their imagination. But if you come to play Macbeth, to study it and say to yourself, as an actor should say: '*What does the text mean?*' you will find yourself appalled at how little the text says in Macbeth's own part which will enable you to build up this great, terrifying figure. I have not re-read Bradley on Macbeth and perhaps I am doing him an injustice if I suggest that it was he who was principally responsible for suggesting that in the last act we find a Macbeth who is something of a philosopher, but it is a notion very widely held that the 'Tomorrow and tomorrow and tomorrow' speech is a philosophical statement. But let me remind you what exactly it says:

> Tomorrow, and tomorrow, and tomorrow,
> Creepes in this petty pace from day to day,
> To the last Syllable of Recorded time:
> And all our yesterdayes, have lighted Fooles
> The way to dusty death. Out, out, breefe Candle,
> Life's but a walking Shadow, a poore Player,
> That struts and frets his houre upon the Stage,
> And then is heard no more. It is a Tale
> Told by an Ideot, full of sound and fury,
> Signifying nothing.
>
> (Act v, scene 5)

There is one overall meaning of this speech and that is this: life has no meaning. If that is a philosophical statement it can only be considered so in a negative or nihilist sense. In point of fact the

Above, MR HORNER in *The Country Wife*, with Edith Evans, Iris Hoey and Eileen Peel: Old Vic, 1936. *Right*, HAMLET: Old Vic Theatre Company, Kronborg Castle, Elsinore, 1950.

BARON TUSENBACH in *The Three Sisters*: Queen's Theatre, 1936. *Left to right*: Peggy Ashcroft, Marie Wright, John Gielgud, Frederick Lloyd (*in foreground*), Barbara Dillon, Leon Quartermaine, Gwen Ffrangcon-Davies, Carol Goodner, Michael Redgrave, Glen Byam Shaw, Harry Andrews, Alec Guinness, George Devine, Angela Baddeley.

speech is a blasphemy, the greatest blasphemy that man can utter.

I remember when I was about to appear as Macbeth, spending some hours with Sir Lewis Casson, who has played and staged Macbeth as often as any other living actor, and saying to him that I could find none of the noble resignation, the philosophy which, as I imagined, I was expected to find in the part, and he said: 'You are quite right and if you will have the courage to do that as you see it, fully believing it, you will be doing something wonderful.' And he pointed out that Macbeth having thus blasphemed against God, calling God an idiot, it might be said that God 'answers back' in the way that would strike most terror into Macbeth's heart – with the news that Birnam Wood has begun to move, which immediately follows the speech that I have just quoted. Macbeth dies, if you follow the text, wishing to bring the world down with him:

  I ginne to be aweary of the Sun,
  And wish th' estate o' th' world were now undon.

and

  At least wee'll dye with Harnesse on our backe

(Act v, scene 7)

And as for his nobility as a soldier, we must not forget that he is ready to fight with Macduff believing himself to be invincible, but from the moment Macduff tells him that he was from his mother's womb untimely ripped Macbeth says: 'I will not fight with thee.'

Another quality often attributed to Macbeth is the quality of being a poet and it is a quality that is very often and quite wantonly, even ridiculously, to my mind, bestowed on many of Shakespeare's leading characters. (It is only true if we say that they are all 'poets'). But here again there is often nothing in the lines themselves to suggest that the character is either consciously or unconsciously making poetry. It is just that Shakespeare clothed his characters in poetry and gave them poetry to utter. A 'First Lord' in *All's Well that Ends Well* can speak the memorable line:

> The webbe of our life, is of a mingled yarne
> good and ill together:
>
> (Act iv, scene 3)

The Queen in *Hamlet* might be considered a poetess when she utters her extravagantly detailed account of Ophelia's death. I would even be prepared to say that Shakespeare would have been astonished at C. E. Montague's suggestion that Richard II is a conscious artist (a theory that several critics of our production have specifically mentioned), in spite of Richard's lengthy and involved flights of rhetoric, some of which contain dazzling poetry. It is not until the deposition and the death scene that there are actual lines which show Richard being conscious of himself as an artist – or might we not say as an actor? And if you are to show Richard as a conscious artist before these scenes, why not show Gaunt and Bolingbroke as conscious artists in the scene of Bolingbroke's farewell?

GAUNT
The sullen passage of thy weary steppes
Esteeme a soyle, wherein thou art to set
The precious Jewell of thy home returne.

BOLINGBROKE
Nay, rather every tedious stride I make,
Will but remember me what a deale of world
I wander from the Jewels that I love.

Must I not serve a long apprentishood,
To forreine passages, and in the end,
Having my freedome, boast of nothing else,
But that I was a journeyman to griefe.

GAUNT

All places that the eie of heaven visits,
Are to a wiseman portes and happie havens:
Teach thy necessity to reason thus,
There is no vertue like necessity,
Thinke not the King did banish thee,
But thou the King: Woe doth the heavier sit,
Where it perceives it is but faintly borne:
Go, say I sent thee foorth to purchase honour,
And not the King exilde thee; or suppose
Devouring pestilence hangs in our aire,
And thou art flying to a fresher clime:
Looke what thy soule holds deare, imagine it
To ly that way thou goest, not whence thou comst:
Suppose the singing birds musitions,
The grasses whereon thou treadst, the presence strowd,
The flowers, faire Ladies, and thy steps, no more
Then a delightfull measure or a dance,
For gnarling sorrow hath lesse power to bite,
The man that mocks at it, and set it light.

BOLINGBROKE

Oh who can hold a fire in his hand
By thinking on the frostie Caucasus? . . .

(Act i, scene 3)

And so on.
This is, of course, poetry; almost as good – though not quite

– as Richard utters. We might as well say that Berowne is a conscious artist, yet his lines excel those of the other courtiers and nobles of *Love's Labour's Lost* only in degree, not in kind.

I have already mentioned an extremely interesting book which appeared recently on Elizabethan acting.[1] In this the author shows very clearly and, I think, convincingly, that Elizabethan actors, like all the literate part of their audiences, had been trained in the art of rhetoric and that they had also possibly set gestures to illustrate certain emotions. The actor's art, he contends, was in many ways identical with that of the orator.

Now, as you know, there is a large body of people who believe that we shall never see Shakespeare's plays as he intended them to be seen unless we revert to a model of the Globe Theatre rebuilt today. I myself only wish that this could be done in order to show its limitations. But reading this book on Elizabethan acting makes me think that to return to the Elizabethan playhouse without at the same time trying to recapture a style of acting which bears small relation to our present style of acting would be only an empty gesture. It would take us no nearer the heart of the plays.

Although a greater understanding of the principles of rhetoric is something which might well benefit our actors, would it really be possible to go back to such a style of acting? One scarcely thinks so. Would it even be advisable? Or would it be what Shakespeare himself would want, were he alive today? (Would Bach reject the modern piano or organ?) Surprised and perhaps shocked as Shakespeare might be by some of our modern stage techniques of acting and production, it seems to me, by considering the evidence of the verse of his plays in their chronological order, that after a time he did everything to re-

[1] *Elizabethan Acting* by B. L. JOSEPH (Oxford University Press, 1950).

duce the rhetorical style and to make it, in some of his later plays, almost impossible for an actor so to declaim. If we take the rhymed couplets of, say *Love's Labour's Lost* or even *Richard II*, it is clear that these cannot be carelessly delivered without a great loss of effect as well as style, but if you glance even casually through the plays in chronological order, it is notable that the big set speeches, when they occur, are more and more involved, the rhythms of them are sometimes smooth and subtle, sometimes, it seems deliberately, choppy.

There is a school of thought that believes that not only must the beat of the verse be kept alive (which most certainly it should be) but that the end of each line should by some means be marked, that is not necessarily to say by a pause, however slight, but by giving a degree of extra weight to the final words of each line. If you study the delivery of the verse from the earlier plays closely, you will see that in 99 times out of 100 this is possible and we may therefore suppose that it was intended to be done. Of the early middle period, as in, for instance, the two parts of *Henry IV*, the verse is so written that it is very difficult not to observe the ends of lines to some extent. For instance, to take a convenient example, Hotspur's long first speech, in which the line overruns only about three times. But when we get to some of the later plays, it becomes the rule rather than the exception that the lines should overrun and finally, in the last plays of all – and I refer principally to the problem plays of the last period, *Timon of Athens, Cymbeline, The Winter's Tale* and *The Tempest* – it becomes almost impossible except for someone with an exceptionally strong photographic memory to memorise the lines in the shape in which they are written.

When I start to study a Shakespearean part I always try to

learn the lines in a rather formal way, for it seems to me that unless you learn the lines so that you could write them out again in more or less the same way that they were written you cannot be expected to do justice to the verse. But I must confess that I would find it very hard to write out from memory the whole of the part of Prospero and find that I had shaped it, line for line, clearly. Many of the speeches, certainly, I could, since I know that they begin with a complete line. I could work them out measure for measure and the result would be tolerably accurate. But have you noticed the number of lines in *The Tempest* which conclude with the word 'and' – a conjunction which it is fairly safe to say should certainly never be stressed in Shakespearean verse? Here are a few examples from Scene 2:

> Had I byn any God of power, I would
> Have suncke the Sea within the Earth, or ere
> It should the good Ship so have swallow'd, and
> The fraughting Soules within her.

There is no earthly reason from the point of view of either scansion or sense that the last foot of the first line, 'I would,' should not complete a line in the next four feet, and the same principle holds for the next two lines.

> Of thee my deere one; thee my daughter who
> Art ignorant of what thou art.
> I doe not thinke thou canst, for then thou was't not
> Out three yeeres old...
> Being once perfected how to graunt suites, ... etc.

These examples are rather tedious to give verbally, but you can easily multiply them for yourselves by glancing again at the texts of later plays.

Is one to suppose that Shakespeare had somehow lost the knack of writing down verses in more or less orderly lengths of iambic pentameters? That is inconceivable, for there is nothing easier than to write iambic pentameters as such once one has the knack of it. Actors, 'winging it,' have been known to invent them. Whatever one might feel about these plays, it is more than unlikely that these line-endings can have been the result of carelessness, and the deduction is obvious: Shakespeare's ear tired of endless iambic pentameters. He tired also of the monotony which actors, professional and amateur, often give to the utterance of them, and more and more he devised means to break the monotony of the verse form and the actors' delivery of it. But perhaps you will say that the speeches are still rhetorical in essence and that the verse form does not affect the rhetoric. You may be right but I think it affects the rhetoric a great deal, for it is extremely difficult, in *The Tempest* at any rate, which is the only one of the late plays of which I have working knowledge, to achieve any kind of sure-fire rhetoric effect (except on certain occasions such as 'Ye elves of hills'). It is as if Shakespeare was there at one's elbow saying 'Get on with it,' or 'Don't try and make too much of that.' I am not putting forward this slight and inadequate resumé of Shakespeare's verse development as anything new or original. Plainly, the early plays were meant to be spoken in one manner and the later plays in another. But I bring it forward rather as an indication of the unending difficulties of the actor's task.

Another trap besetting the modern actor of Shakespeare is that he has grown up in an age of drama which is preponderantly naturalistic, which not only unfits him for the somewhat larger projection which is required for Shakespeare's characters but which makes him search for a number of psychological motives which Shakespeare has been at no pains to supply. As much has been written about *Othello* as about any other of the great plays.

Yet has anyone really satisfactorily found the reason of Iago's villainy to an extent that is clear to us all? And what is true of Iago is true of a number of other characters, large and small. It is very difficult, for instance, when you are playing Horatio, to know what Horatio thinks at the moment when Ophelia's funeral comes into sight, for we have seen Horatio, presumably resident at Elsinore, receiving letters from Hamlet and indeed, in one version of the play, being present during Ophelia's mad scene. And yet he says nothing to warn his friend the Prince that the approaching funeral is that of Hamlet's late betrothed. We, the audience, do not notice this. But the modern, more psychological actor may be teased by it. He is wrong, of course. All that counts in the theatre is what the audience receives.

The impact of the great Russian producer Stanislavski upon all Western acting has been of incomputable force. Like Craig or Bradley, but in a much more forceful way, he has influenced thousands of actors and producers who may never have seen his work or even read his books. In so far as Stanislavski's chief insistence might be said to be an insistence for truth of feeling and emotion, it has been a healthy influence, for it has worked against what is often the bad fairy of the theatre: effect for effect's sake. But in so far as Stanislavski's theory of acting (the most complete that the world has yet known) has led actors to try to express sub-conscious truth which can all too easily become merely subjective truth, his method, misunderstood and misinterpreted at several removes, has also done much harm, as many good and true things are capable of doing if they are misreported. Perhaps the most famous of all theories and surely the most often quoted is Hamlet's advice to the players (Act iii, scene 2), with its insistence that the end and the purpose of playing, both at the first and now, was and is 'to hold as 'twer a Mirrour up to Nature; to shew Vertue her owne Feature, Scorne her owne Image, and the very Age and Bodie of the Time, his forme and pressure.'

The history of actors since Shakespeare's time – and that is, roughly speaking, the full history of all the English actors we know – has praised each succeeding great actor for his truth and closeness to nature. And there can be no doubt that Shakespeare meant every word of what he said in Hamlet's advice to the players, though I have often noted the significance of the replies made by the First Player, a man, be it noted, whom Hamlet had praised for his performance of Aeneas' Tale to Dido. He makes only two remarks and they are very brief.

> I warrant your Honor

is one and the second

> I hope we have reform'd that indifferently with us, Sir.

In life, Hamlet's advice to the players would seem somewhat insulting even to a mediocre actor, yet we do not feel that it is insulting when we see it played in the theatre and we are not meant to. Shakespeare is serving up to the public the public's favourite idea about acting – that it should be 'natural,' 'lifelike,' with a few additional lines of seemingly, technical advice, such as:

> Nor do not saw the ayre too much with your hand thus

and

> There bee Players that I have seene Play ... that have so strutted and bellowed ...

which are no more than opportunities for the actor who plays Hamlet to mock a bad actor and by contrast show how 'natural' he is himself being.

Of course the advice to the players is a great scene and provides a superb opportunity for more or less effective display by the actor who plays Hamlet. But to my mind the most significant remark on acting occurs in an earlier scene, when Hamlet, inviting the first player to recite says:

> Wee'l e'ne to't like French Faulconers, fly at anything we see: wee'l have a Speech straight.

In that line, I suggest – though you may think the theory a little far-fetched – is the key to what should be and very often is the actor's attitude towards acting Shakespeare.

Given an almost unbelievable scene of extreme jealousy (I am not thinking here so much of Othello as of Leontes), Shakespearean actors should be able to go to it like French falconers and act, quite simply, 'jealousy.' Shakespeare supplies them with superb words and leaves them to get on with it. The same is true of the actors' difficulties with the start of Macbeth. It holds also in the most unconvincingly prepared change of heart and act of forgiveness of Prospero. Shakespeare, although he undoubtedly wrote some characters which were consistent and psychologically true in detail, did so for the sake of contrast and because, strangely enough, it is much easier to write naturalistic characters, about whom there are few questions to be asked, than it is to write the Macbeths, the Hamlets, the Othellos, the Lears and even the Leontes and the Prosperos. It is as easy comparatively as to write metrically perfect iambic pentameters.

A large part of Shakespeare's stage craft is impressionistic. It is impressionistic, we know, in the setting of scene and atmosphere. (That is obvious: 'The air bites shrewdly, it is very cold,' etc.) But I do not remember seeing it suggested elsewhere that Shakespeare also extended this impressionistic technique to some of his greater characters, who, it is generally supposed, are teeming with psychological subtleties, all of which can be reconciled by ingenious theories to make half-a-dozen or, as in the case of Hamlet, a dozen different things. We can, if we wish, produce a theory, as Dr. Ernest Jones has done, that Hamlet loved his mother. When we read Dr. Jones the theory is extremely plausible. But I think he omits to mention that Hamlet never refers to his mother with one endearing phrase and that all his phrases of filial love are directed towards the memory of his father. You can read into Hamlet that he was a Spanish nobleman, a man of action seeking revenge, which I believe is Señor de Madariaga's theory. It would take a month of Sundays to relate all the theories that have been made of Hamlet and of all the other great characters. I am not suggesting that all the obscurities of these characters are due to our failure to see that the characters are not meant to be realistic. I think we must allow Shakespeare some margin of error, too. The artist who is prodigious in creation is often poor at revision. We know from Ben Jonson that he wrote hurriedly and sometimes carelessly and we can also guess that if he had had the time or patience to make thorough revision, half the scholars' labours of comparing Quarto and Folio, of inventing stage directions which he may have given his actors by word of mouth, and so on, would never have been needed.

The actor's task with Shakespeare is to bring the plays theatrically to life. (I mean theatrically in its pure sense and not its debased one.) The plays only come fully to life – despite our latter-day Charles Lambs – in the theatre. No actor can hope for a success of perfection. No audience should demand it. The plays themselves, although among the highest manifestations of human genius, are imperfect, perhaps by very reason of their blessed humanity. In one sense, Matthew Arnold was wrong: even Shakespeare abides our question. If he did not, we should not love him so much.

ACTORS AND AUDIENCES

IN THE DAYS when Dame Marie Tempest was in her heyday – which for the purposes of this discussion might be said to be every night of her long career as a star – it is said that a strip of fresh white drugget was laid at the side of the stage, leading to a little row of chairs with fresh white chair-covers for the ladies of the company to sit on. This was no mere formality. It was to assure that the ladies' evening dresses and even their shoes should be spotless when they made their entrances. A younger actress has assured me that Dame Marie, who, like the few women who attain pre-eminence in the theatre and manage to keep it, was a strict disciplinarian, would wag an admonitory finger at the girl who strayed from this white path of probity. Such precautions may be thought to be excessive and can hardly be said to obtain in England today. More's the pity, for it is only in the framework of a strictly disciplined company that good working conditions, in which the actor's spirit flourishes, can be found. If anyone thinks that that is a new-fangled notion, let him read Macready's diaries and see how he tried to obtain reasonable conditions for himself and his fellow actors and how miserable he became when thwarted.

No member of the audience could or indeed should realise the number of factors which can influence for the evening the player's freedom and the delight of the spectators. But there they are, and on this side of the curtain they cannot be ignored.

* * *

It is a night of this year and I find myself coming upstairs after Act ii with Diana Wynyard. She is wearing a cocoon of a cheap white cotton cloak, to keep her expensive white evening dress looking exquisite – a precaution for which a generation brought up on the dubious efficacy of a '24-hour' dry-cleaning service and mass-produced clothes has little time. We catch each other's eye and, because I feel ready to burst, I say, crossing my fingers, (we actors are superstitious) 'I'm not imagining it, am I?' She knows what I mean but, also superstitiously, queries: 'What?' I blurt it out: 'This feeling of . . . you know . . . complete communication.' She nods, her eyes shining. We both agree, with a laugh, that Act iii will probably be disaster. We do not feel secure in feeling so free to feel secure. It is not often one feels so secure with a fellow-player as to mention such a thing.

Act iii, perhaps because of this, perhaps in spite of it, seems to go as seldom before.

It is that rare, all too rare occasion, when the actor feels he can do no wrong. It is like sailing in a good breeze. The shape of the land, the depth of the water, everything becomes clear. No hurried glances to the shore, no last-minute calculation, no sense of danger. There is no fear of the often predictable but avoidable nervous laugh which may ruin a tense scene, no need to try to kill the inapt round on a final exit. The audience is not merely held by the actors; it seems to cradle them in its arms.

This is, for the player, rare and rewarding. It is, as they say, something to write home about. But what is the good of writing home or anywhere else? Not only is the reception at the end seemingly identical with last Saturday's, but even a constant playgoer would scarcely know where the differences lay. He will notice a difference, if he is sensitive, and that is all. Analyse it? It would be wrong if he had to do so.

It would be equally wrong if the player were to believe that there is no difference.

Every experienced actor knows the danger which accompanies enjoyment in acting. But it should be enjoyed just the same. The relationship of actor to audience is as precarious as a love affair. There must always be one who kisses and one who turns the cheek. There can be no doubt, if you come to think of it, whose rôle is which.

* * *

We often say that a play is not a play until it is acted, and acted before an audience. It must be confessed, however, that to the actor the truism could often – not of course always or finally – end with the words 'until it is acted,' a limitation which would leave out the potential audience entirely. For it is true that many of the most exciting and true moments of the actor's work come during rehearsals. Then it is that the creative mood, the instinct which makes an actor say a certain line in a certain way, the impulse which prompts a certain perhaps 'unforgettable' gesture, burns brightly though fitfully. The process whereby the actor begins to be able to identify himself with the part is one of the most absorbing of all his work. I do not mean to suggest that once rehearsals are over the creative mood can be hung up on a mental coathanger; for the actor's chief and abiding problem is to find the creative mood by which he can persuade the audience that he is such or such a character and that the things he says and does are being said and done for the first time every night. He must find this creative mood every night without fail. The actor's performances may vary, and they certainly do, according to the degree to which he has been able to find it. During the run of a play, some of the moments to which I referred before, moments when the actor suddenly perceives how a line should be said or how a move should be made, are multiplied, sometimes beyond expectation. But some of them are never quite the same as when, during that concentrated excitement of rehearsals, they were first created.

I do not think with good professional actors that the performances vary in any marked manner. But there can be and often is a shift of emphasis, a tightening up or, more probably, a relaxation all of which can make deep differences to the persuasive powers of a performance. And surely it is persuasion which comes first in the actor's armoury? He must persuade the audience to suspend its disbelief. But the fact must be faced, especially in the performances of great parts, that an accumulation of tiny differences due to the elusiveness of the creative mood can make Wednesday evening's performance much more persuasive than that of Tuesday evening. Mounet-Sully, the great French tragedian, would say quite simply on some occasions: 'Ce soir le Dieu n'est pas venu.' Louis Jouvet, a highly intellectual and technical as well as a great actor, said that there were certain evenings on which one might expect 'cette grâce.' Only what I would call the real playgoers, the ones who come to see the plays and performances they like more than once and who sometimes come again and again can understand this. It is not that when the God does not come and there is no dispensation of grace the performance is necessarily bad. It may be good, even exciting, and it may have wonderful moments, but it can lack that essence which Stendhal, writing on the subject of love, called crystallization. We therefore do not fall in love with it, we are not swept off our feet, however much we may admire. The responsibility for creating this love affair must, of course, be the actor's.

But not entirely. The actor may go astray in technique, or through lack of feeling, or sometimes even through too much feeling – or rather shall we say through a failure to control and project what he feels. The audience, on the other hand, can miss the point for a variety of causes, and some of these the audience brings with it to the theatre. At theatres like the Old Vic or the Memorial Theatre at Stratford a certain number of each audience comes to a play with at least a rough working knowledge of the text, and then always we actors sense that perhaps there is someone whose judgement, in Hamlet's words, 'must o'erweigh a whole theatre of others' – who possibly knows more about the text than we actors do, we who have merely studied it and learnt it by heart and lent to it what personality or talent we may possess and which may sometimes seem quite irrelevant to its nature. The actor's relationship to a well-known rôle must often seem, to true lovers of Shakespeare, like what might be called a whirlwind courtship, or, what is even less convincing, a *mariage de convenance*, the one unlikely to last and the other false at heart.

As an audience, we readily assume that something that is really interesting will be bound to interest us, or that something that is really moving cannot fail to move us. If we are not interested or excited we assume it is dull. Here we can fool ourselves. There are a hundred thousand reasons why, at any given moment, we should fail to respond. Private associations of thought; some personal problem which, seemingly pushed to the back of the mind, yet insists on pushing itself to the front; some mental or physical like or dislike: the colour of someone's hair, a preconception about the height, girth or even the colour of the eyes, some antipathy to a certain subject or line of thought of which we may be quite unconscious ourselves can cause us, in the

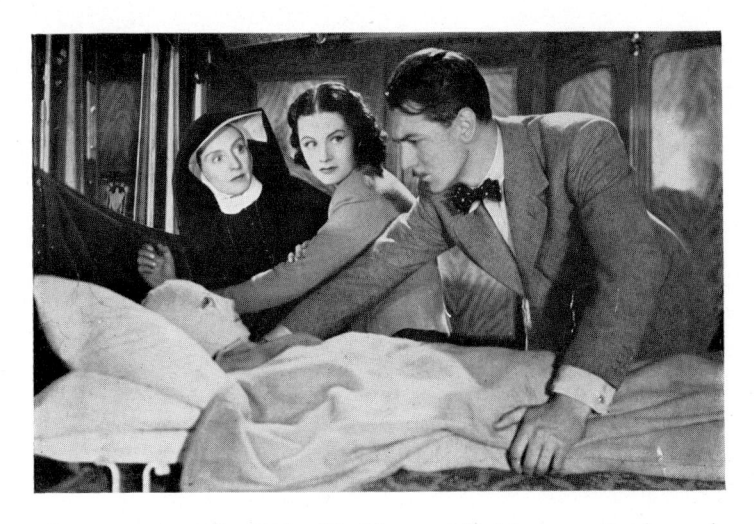

GILBERT in *The Lady Vanishes*, with Margaret Lockwood and Catherine Lacey: directed by Alfred Hitchcock, 1938.

Left, KIPPS, with Diana Wynyard: directed by Carol Reed, 1940. *Right*, ALAN MACKENZIE in *Stolen Life*, with Elizabeth Bergner: directed by Paul Czinner, 1938.

Left, on the set with Cavalcanti during the filming of *Dead of Night*, 1944. *Right*, ORIN MANNON in *Mourning becomes Electra*, with Nancy Coleman, Kirk Douglas and Katina Paxinou: directed by Dudley Nichols, 1952.

theatre as in life, quite simply, to 'miss the point.' Then, also – as King Lear says – 'We are not ourselves when nature, being oppressed, commands the mind to suffer with the body.' Common knowledge, as well as the statistics of the National Health Service, would support Lear's view, and without delving into those statistics I think we can assume that a large percentage of the average audience (though every actor knows there is no such thing as an average audience) comes to the theatre ailing in body; I do not mean, of course, those who occasionally come in wheel-chairs or on sticks, for such invalids, to get themselves to a theatre at all, bring with them an almost sacrificial attention. I do not mean someone behind you with the churchyard cough who, it is charitable to suppose, would be far better off in bed. I do not mean the man in whom a mysterious allergy (the smell of theatre-programmes?) produces a succession of thunder-and-lightning sternutations, though I would remind him that if, unexpectedly, the actor pulls a pistol out of his pocket, the poor wretch will at once stop sneezing. I mean those whose ailments may be no more than slight hunger or mild indigestion. Or addiction; for think of the victim who cannot see a cigarette on the stage without compulsively clutching his lighter! I mean also that vast majority of people who, alas! do not see or do not hear nearly so well as they think they do. Nowadays, when the Health Service provides even the people who do not need them with attractive glasses it seems a pity that hearing-aids are still considered sexually unattractive.

However, I am not encouraging you to jump to the conclusion that these circumstances – which cannot be more than adduced – are irremediable. The theatre is in itself a remedy. The commonest cliché of theatrical criticism is that the audience comes to the theatre to enjoy themselves and not to think. That is quite true, though it should be added that there is sometimes much enjoyment to be got out of thinking. Even the simpler-minded members of the audience can, and frequently do, exclaim 'How true that is!'

I get tired of a certain word very frequently used nowadays. It has a meaning in its strict sense but as commonly used it is so debased that it has none. What is commonly called 'escapist' should often be called 'remedial.' The theatre is perhaps the most potent remedy for passing ailments. I do not mean the plays of an Ibsen or a Shaw, which helped to remedy ailments that are more than what might be called passing – even if some of them have now passed – or a Sophocles or a Shakespeare whose works are remedies in the degree that food, love and sunshine are remedies. No, the theatre is indeed in any sense a remedy; for, to use an old-fashioned jargon, we go to it to forget ourselves. Or, as we say now, to relax. 'To relax': it sounds so futile, feeble – fatuous, even. Yet you do not have to be a Yogi to know that nothing is accomplished without relaxation.

There is a phrase with which an older generation of actors were familiar: 'Doctor Theatre.' Every actor or actress who may have been physically ailing during the day, or mentally depressed, tired or even worried finds that from the moment he or she steps on the stage the worry or ailment is more or less forgotten, the pain can vanish, years can drop from our back. It has been described how Ellen Terry, with old age at hand and eyesight nearly gone, could come stumblingly and cautiously to the wings and, on her cue, would lift her head, smile, shed most of her years like a cloak and seem to dance on to the stage.

I remember myself, when playing Macbeth in New York, being temporarily lame to the point where I had, as I thought, to use a stick to get from a car to my dressing room and from the dressing room to the stage. Well, of course, you cannot play Macbeth with a stick (though I can think of at least one producer who might even think Macbeth as a cripple 'rather amusing') so I would enter without the stick, walking up and down the complicated and uneven steps of our rostrums with scarcely apparent difficulty. Sometimes, especially when it came to the fight, I was conscious that I had to shift my weight from one leg to the other, but when it came to Macbeth's death fall I could not, at any performance, 'save myself,' because I knew it was a good fall and my actor's vanity overcame any desire to protect myself. I very well remember that as I came to the wings again, where my dresser was waiting for me with my stick, I shooed him aside, whispering 'No, I am sure I can do without that now.' But I could not. After a few steps my lameness overcame me again, and it was hard to believe how I had got through the last scene. 'Doctor Theatre,' though an uncanny practitioner, has a limited practice.

* * *

So much, and all too inadequately, for the remedial powers of the theatre. I deliberately used the word remedial and not the word social, for it is the remedy that is common to both actor and audience. As I have said, every actor knows that there is no such thing as an average audience, and certainly no spectator ever thinks that he is part of such a thing, for one of the great powers of the theatre is that it is able to persuade each member of its audience that what is about to happen is about to happen because a number of people are specially gathered there to see it. And perhaps it is only people who are more or less completely extrovert who do not unconsciously feel that it is all happening for them. I do not mean that each spectator imagines himself a

Ludwig of Bavaria, who would command performances in the private theatre of his castle, to which even the ladies and gentlemen of his Court were not invited, but that each audience arrives at the theatre with such a variety of preconceptions, such assorted anticipations and, in some cases, such an armoury of prejudices, all slightly different each night, that it is something of a miracle that the theatre can ever reconcile or satisfy these prejudices and anticipations.

That it does so is common knowledge. It is the chief function of the theatre. Occasions like the first night of *The Playboy of the Western World* at the Abbey Theatre which set the audience fighting each other are, fortunately for the box office, and perhaps unhappily for the history of the drama, rare. Scarcely elsewhere in the world other than in Stratford-on-Avon, can there be a theatre where the audience is composed from such various places, races, nationalities, creeds. But that theatre is unique and it is so by the personality and work of one man, Shakespeare. The average play, its author and its performers and its average audiences are not conducted and inspired by such a master, nor framed in such a setting. The extremes of accord and disaccord between actors and audiences can be very marked. In most theatres all over the world a cardinal concern of the actor – and not only if he is a star actor who has a percentage in the gross – can be the size of the 'House.' It is not simply that this affects the weekly pay packet but that it touches the actor's reputation. To the other members of the cast, on their fixed salaries, this is also important since if the bookings seem to be waning for other than well-known reasons such as Christmases and Coronations, their livelihood is threatened, and it is important to remember that all actors, from those who are on a percentage to those with the Equity minimum salary, live as casual labourers.

At least, that is so in this country where, to digress for a moment, the long struggles, lasting over a hundred years, of men like Matthew Arnold, Shaw, William Archer, Granville-Barker and Geoffrey Whitworth to establish a proper National Theatre in the sense that the Comédie Française is a National Theatre have resulted in a theoretical and (in terms of armaments) insignificant million pounds, the laying of a foundation-stone on the South Bank, the shifting of it because the site was wanted for something else, and the resignation and apathy of all but we few, we poor, cranky few.

What we chiefly need in our theatre is a building and a subsidy for that building where the great plays of the world can from season to season be seen in the best possible conditions. It is true that we have such a theatre at Stratford for the plays of Shakespeare, but we must admit that without the attraction of Shakespeare's town and birthplace and the charm of the Warwickshire countryside and many other contributory factors, that theatre, however well run, would not pay its way. To present the plays of the world in a style adequate for a National Theatre, Granville-Barker, many years ago now, anticipated that a preliminary subsidy of a million pounds was necessary, but he also stipulated that a National Theatre would need more than one stage – a small auditorium as well as a large one – an idea which has been thought of and carried into practice in almost every large town in Scandinavia and Germany. It is pointless to try to present, say, Ibsen's *The Doll's House* on a stage that is adequate for a full scale modern production of *Julius Caesar*. Barker envisaged a permanent company of about seventy with enough leading actors and actresses and 'featured players' as would remove some of the mistakes of repertory casting. A site must be chosen, he said, with adequate room for storage space, wardrobe, dressing rooms, rehearsal rooms and so planned that these central facilities of each were equally available to the two joint houses.

'Who wants such a place?' cry those sections of the press who keep worrying about 'The tax-payers money,' as if it were the widow's mite. Who wanted the Old Vic? Emma Cons and Lilian Baylis wanted it. Now, even those who don't go to it realise it has to be there.

* * *

Revenons à nos patrons. The audience arrives at the theatre, unconsciously, I suggest, bristling with prejudices. It will have read in the press comments about the play which, even if all favourable – a most unlikely contingency – would seem to cancel each other out. If it has not read these it may have heard tell of reports on the play and performances which are equally contradictory. Indeed, in the conditions under which dramatic critics have to work, they are bound to be so. The weekly and Sunday papers have time to see the whole play but often the daily papers have to telephone their reports some time before the play is over. An actor's views on dramatic critics are naturally suspect and I have noticed, looking back over the notices of plays which I have done long since, that what at the time had seemed to me a harsh or even savage press was not, in tone, so far off the mark of what one eventually came to feel about the production oneself. Though we remember certain phrases of outstanding praise, we tend to take a number of other compliments for granted and only the sharper barbs of the slings and arrows department remain lodged under our skin. I do not want you to take this as an example of the well-known 'actor's vanity.' Actors do not have a monopoly of vanity. I have known barristers, doctors, lawyers, hotel keepers and journalists and critics themselves show hypersensitivity to criticism of their work. It is *while you are doing it* that you mind, and one of the reasons why you mind is that you are doing it in front of an audience, many of whom, you cannot help assuming, have read this, that or the other, and have come in a mood which means, if not exactly in so many words, 'Prove it' or 'Show us.' This may seem not only hypersensitive but fatuous of the actor, since he can equally well assume, you may well say, that if people have bought their tickets with solid cash they have solid reasons for wishing to see the play.

As I said, an audience arrives at the theatre at Stratford-on-Avon with rather more than the common bond which links an audience together. Consciously or unconsciously – and without venturing into the shallow rapids of that dangerous term 'highbrow' – audiences drawn, as I say, from all over the world come to see Shakespeare's plays at Stratford-on-Avon with an extra sense of expecting something more (or rather, something else) than they can get at even the most exciting production in other theatres. Some of them come with a sense of dedication. Quite a few, I am sure, come with a feeling of penance. As a gentleman was heard to remark leaving that theatre one night after one or other of the 'tragedies': 'Every bloody play I come to now seems to last more than three hours.' Then, too, quite a number of people come, some of whom never come again, having perhaps some sense of expiation but not the least idea of what to expect. It sometimes astonishes me that the genius of Shakespeare and the combined skill of the director and actors should succeed in keeping such members of the audience quiet, let alone satisfying them. For really, a number of them have so little idea of what is in store for them that I can well believe the story which was told me by members of the Sadler's Wells Ballet Company who were performing at that theatre for a fortnight before Dame Peggy Ashcroft and I opened there in *The Merchant of Venice*. Two ladies were reading their programmes for the Ballet *Coppelia*, and one said to the other: 'Oh dear! We've picked the wrong day. Peggy Ashcroft and Michael Redgrave aren't dancing.' You or I, of course, would never do such a thing, and perhaps it is one of the things on which we may justifiably pride ourselves.

Fortunately for us actors the majority of every audience in every theatre has – or so one hopes – a better idea of what to expect. But we must consider the fact that a great many people not only do not go to the theatre regularly but never go to the theatre at all throughout their lives. This is sometimes because they have no possible opportunity, living say, in some valley in Wales where to visit the nearest big town (and how many of these now have theatres?) represents a day's shopping expedition and no more. There are others who have never acquired a real taste for the theatre even when it is at their doorstep. I am not thinking of certain inhabitants of Stratford who like to pretend that they can never get into the theatre because the tickets are all sold to Americans when what they really mean is that they don't want to go to the theatre anyway and are sick to death of the sound of Shakespeare's name and the sight of his bust on a box of chocolate biscuits. I am thinking rather of a don whom I met in the common room of an Oxford College where I was lunching during a week when I was playing at one of the local theatres. The Master politely introduced me to this don and explained: 'Mr. Redgrave is playing at the New Theatre this week.' The don struggled towards polite small-talk rather as a drowning man might struggle towards the surface and uttered very slowly a sentence which I shall never forget: 'Ah yes. I am afraid I cannot count myself a very ... er ... staunch ... er ... supporter of the theatre. I have only been to one four times in my life.' Since he was well into his seventies, I could not feel that he would have contributed greatly to the audience's enjoyment and I was rather glad to feel that whatever those four occasions were, I had not had to take part in them. For it is perfectly possible for even one member of the audience to cause a kind of short-circuit in the receptivity and response of the rest of the audience. Many of you must have noticed this from time to time: how one man, or a couple, or a small group of friends, though they have presumably paid for their seats and come to the theatre with the same motive that has induced us there, namely enjoyment, so signally fail to enjoy themselves that without barracking, without hissing, without loud or muttered exclamations of disapproval, he, she or they can create around them widening circles of disapproval or chilly dislike. I myself, I must confess, have not only seen this phenomenon as a spectator in front – a phenomenon which is indicated by nothing more, it may be, than a rigid head and shoulders and a complete absence of any reaction whatever – but I have felt myself part of it when at a performance which I have not only not enjoyed but actively disliked. On such occasions I find that my chin is sinking lower and lower on to my chest and that I am squinting at the play out of the corner of my eyes as if to take in as little as possible. That is the first stage with me. The second and dangerous stage is when my head begins to roll from side to side like a tethered animal and the third stage is my exit from the theatre, for I am not one of those cussed people who, because I have paid my money, will stay to the end to torture myself. Nor, obviously, is it permitted for me to boo and, indeed, I have never had any inclination to do so. But then, I am not a typical audience. No artist is. I can sometimes enjoy a play I know to be bad. I can admit to seeing things through my heart, which is not the same, whatever anybody may say, as sentimentality. I can also admit, as one who registers his sense of awareness by the hour, that one can be suffering from a simple lack of response.

As for booing and similar demonstrations, sociologists would have us believe that it is, at least, 'positive' and therefore a healthy sign of vitality in the audience. I wonder. The theatre on the whole is a civilising influence and I think it should be taken on civil terms. I do not want to make any invidious comparisons of the audiences of different nations. Nor do I maintain that a New York theatre audience is the best in the world. But to my mind it is a mark in their favour that if they feel they cannot stay to applaud they do not stay to boo. They do not stay at all. The manager who looks at the house before the third act of a first night in New York and sees that many of the seats have not been reoccupied knows that he has a failure on his hands. It would certainly be foolhardy to make disparagements of the general behaviour of audiences in this country if I were to compare them unfavourably with other countries, nor do I wish to do so. Audiences are different from country to country just as they are from night to night. And although I have enormously enjoyed some receptions on the continent which seemed like bigger ovations than English audiences tend to give, we must remember that in England, too, we tend to give a louder ovation to the foreign actor. Nevertheless, it is pleasant to bring an audience literally to its feet – or to have them, sitting outside a nearby café or in a restaurant after the show, break into applause – that is to say to have them wish to stand to show how much they have enjoyed a performance. And I have on occasions noticed in England that the intrepid party which ventures to stand up to applaud is greeted with cries of 'Sit down.' There are very few English men or women who will venture to shout out the accolade 'bravo!' It just does not seem to be in our temperament and it is perhaps significant that we have no native word for 'bravo' or 'encore'? When we do bestow these they seem strangled in our throats. Personally I do it myself when I can sincerely feel like doing so, for I know what joy it gives to the performer to have even one voice calling out, but here again discretion is the better part of *chaleur*. If the piece is a flop the lone champion can sound either like a raven or a backer. 'Nevermore!' or 'No more dough!' Anyway, I entirely approve of Irving's subterfuge with his kettledrums[1] for it shows how well he understood his fellow countrymen. On the other hand, I heartily detest the thought of a *claque*, as Chaliapin did when he first sang in Milan and booted the leader of a *claque* down the stairs.[2]

A *claque* is the lowest form of *clique*. I find it interesting to discover that the onomatopœic *claque* can mean the crack of a whip (or some other dry sound) and that a secondary meaning of *clique*, according to Larousse, is an ensemble of bugles and side drums. To remember, also, that Chaliapin said in Milan 'The voice of the audience was like the touch of the whip to a racehorse.'

Dr. Johnson's couplet
> The Drama's laws the Drama's patrons give
> For we who live to please must please to live

is usually, like most resounding couplets, thought to be a bullseye but like similar paradoxes it only elevates a half-truth above

[1] See page 34.
[2] See *The Times* 12 September 1957.

its station, for it is no more true of the actor than of the creative artist that he should be preoccupied with a desire to please everybody. The one person he must please above all else is himself. A dangerous conceit, it might appear, but the phrase 'playing to the gallery' has as much meaning as it ever did, even when, thanks to television and the cinema, the gallery seats are the last to be filled.

This is a somewhat slippery subject for an actor to speak about for I remember a good friend of mine at Cambridge, a don who was especially interested in drama and the theatre, a brilliant and sympathetic woman, when I told her of my somewhat belated determination to go on the stage and follow my father's and mother's and grandfather's and grandmother's footsteps, writing to me that she was sorry to hear this and though she wouldn't argue with me she put forward for my consideration the thought that: 'If the volume of applause is the measure of your success how can you avoid making it your aim?' I think I replied, as I thought then and still think now, that though there is more than a germ of truth in this it can be equally applied to many other professions. Equally? No, perhaps not. But in so far as an actor is an artist, and I am proud to say that I truly believe that in the English acting profession, some of those acting leading parts and many of those acting smaller ones, there are many real artists, this stricture does not apply. It is human nature to wish for praise where praise is due and it is also human nature to kick against the pricks. In the matter of actors and audiences the pricks can sometimes be very slight and yet produce grievous consequences.

I wish I were competent to deal in psychological terms with the kind of qualified enthusiasm which, as I suspect, is more latent in this country than in others due to our Puritanism, and which makes so many people who take the trouble to write to thank an actor for his performance feel it necessary to say: 'This is the first time I have ever written to an actor.' They intend to confer, one supposes, a special accolade. Yet frankly, after reading – as most public figures must have done – more letters of this type than I can remember, one cannot help wondering whether some of those writers are not unconsciously praising themselves. Then there are a number of people who wish for a player's autograph but who feel constrained to preface the request with: 'It is for my girl friend,' 'for my wife,' 'for my son' or 'for the friend of a friend.'

It is surely interesting to think what a number of people there must be, if all these requests are literally true, who cannot speak for themselves. For my part, I think I would rather ask for myself than get someone to ask for me and should feel disappointment at obtaining what I wanted only by proxy. Then there is – we cannot avoid this dreadful word any longer – the 'fan' who feels that it would not be seemly to bestow the cloak of praise without the thrust of a small verbal stiletto. Sometimes this dagger takes on the proportions of a broadsword, as for instance when Miss Zena Dare, as she tells me, was met at the stage door at Southport where she had previously appeared in many very successful musical shows but where, on this occasion, she was appearing in a straight play at which the audiences were small. Miss Dare, with her usual acerbity laced with cream, remarked to the admirer who asked for her autograph: 'You don't seem to like straight plays in Southport.' The reply was: 'No, we simply dread them.'

Collecting the remarks of the audience coming out from a show is often a favourite pastime of the actor – visiting the show of his colleagues – and I remember going at least three times to see the memorable revival of *The Seagull* at the New Theatre. In this particular production, Trigorin wore, in the last act, a sort of purplish tweedy suit and on one occasion, as I left the theatre, I heard a lady saying anxiously to the man who was with her, having obviously persuaded him to come against his will: 'Well, dear, how did you like it? Did you jump when the poor young man shot himself? I did.' His answer was blunt and uncompromising: 'Well, if it had been me, I'd have shot the fellow in the purple bags.'

Sometimes – though now I fear I am getting into the stride of a gossip column rather than a serious lecture – sometimes actors do not have to be part of the audience of some other play to hear the reactions of the audience. For instance, at several London theatres it so happens that some of the dressing rooms overhang and can overhear the gallery or pit queue. The comments one hears while making up can sometimes be very dashing, though they are probably none the less salutary. I remember that until the new wing of dressing rooms was built at Stratford, for some mysterious reason which I was never able to fathom – I suggest because it was early closing day – a group of young men and women would assemble by the former stage door to have what one supposes was their weekly theatre chat. I do not think they went into the theatre – though they may have done – because when the half-hour was called they were frequently still talking. Their remarks on the theatre were often devastating. But what I chiefly remember was their predilection for disaster. 'My dear' I remember one of them saying, 'I was there on the night when Flora Robson dried up!' But sometimes one hears equally devastating remarks at a time when one might suppose that one would be immune from them: during performance. I remember when playing in Turgenev's *A Month in the Country* at the St.

James's, settling down for the first undisturbed duologue between the heroine, Natalia Petrovna, and myself and looking up at Miss Valerie Taylor with eyes swimming with affection and love, when I heard a lady in the stalls whisper to someone beside her: 'I like *her*.' I was rather quick on my cues after that.

Very few members of an audience can possibly realise that the auditorium is in many ways a much better sounding board than the stage itself with its wings and borders and gaps which allow even the loudest and clearest voice partially to slide backstage. Much of what is muttered or whispered in an auditorium is not heard by the other members of the audience because for those in the audience who are sitting behind the mutterer the voice is projected away and for those who are sitting in front the shape of the human ear is directed away from it and attention is concentrated on the lighted stage. Funnily – and justly – enough, it is usually at moments when the actor is too pleased with himself that one hears some of these mutterings or whisperings. Again, I remember, when playing Macheath in *The Beggar's Opera* at the Haymarket Theatre, being disturbed to a point where I was for a few moments unable to continue. Macheath has, as you will remember, what we call a well built up entrance. For half an hour or so before he comes on the rest of the cast do little else but talk or sing about him and the director had devised for me a sensational entrance out of a cupboard on a landing, with pistols cocked, a jump over the banisters on to the counter of Peachum's shop and a further drop down on to the stage and straight into the duet 'Pretty Polly, say.' After the duet there is a short spoken scene, then one solo number by Macheath followed by the duet 'Over the hills and far away' and after another duet, 'Oh what pain it is to part,' an exit through a window, a rose and a kiss thrown to Polly. Curtain. The second act opens in a tavern where, after Macheath's gang have sung the opening chorus, Macheath enters, has a short scene with his highwaymen friends and settles down for the first solo that he has alone on the stage, his most charming number, 'If the heart of a man is depressed with cares.' Now it was true that in this production I, as Macheath, had on an overcoat for this second act, but otherwise my costume and make-up were the same. On this particular occasion the orchestra started the introduction to the song and I advanced with painted wine glass in my hand to sit astride a chair in order to sing it. I was careful, of course, to conceal the fact that I was husbanding my breath and, again perhaps I was feeling too pleased with myself, for I felt that I cut a fairly dashing figure. In the tiny pause between the end of the introduction and the beginning of the song I heard a voice whisper in tones worthy of Mrs. Pat Campbell: '*Who* is *this?*' On that particular occasion I lost my breath and a curious kind of snort came out. The conductor looked at me rather surprised and, after I had shaken my head at him like a dumb ox, he started the introduction again, and *The Beggar's Opera* continued.

It is inevitable, perhaps, that the audience should sometimes communicate to the actor some expression of their feelings, however irrelevant these may be. There are those who think that the advent of the talkies, where the voices are magnified and distorted and where obviously the reactions of the audience cannot affect the actor, has something to do with the insensitivity of certain members of the audience in this matter. Personally I do not agree. In my not very long professional career, for what my opinion is worth, I think I have noted a marked increase in the attention and self-control of the audiences. In many cases much of this is due to the increasing prohibition of smoking. It is a simple truth that persistent smokers do not realise how often they cough. The deplorable habit of drinking tea off trays on laps which is so prevalent in English theatres is due, of course, to the fact that so few English theatres have foyers or lounges large enough to accommodate the audience. It was due to a tea drinker that I once lost my temper in the middle of a performance and addressed the audience. It was during a matinée of *A Month in the Country*. After a fifteen minute interval during which teas were being served the second act began with a long soliloquy from the heroine after which I had to enter for an impassioned scene between us both. I could hear, as I stood in the wings, the rattle of tea cups and this annoyed me, more particularly as I had recently complained that fifteen minutes was surely long enough for people to drink their tea and the manager had promised to do something about it. As I waited my irritation mounted and I forced myself to remember what Edith Evans had once told me. She recalled how, when they were playing *The Way of the World*, and the local Hammersmith boys would come and bang on the scene-dock doors out of pure mischief, which used to throw her out of gear, Robert Loraine, seeing her distress, had advised: 'If there is a disturbance which you can stop, have it stopped! If you can't stop it, take no notice!' On this particular occasion I reminded myself of this and said to myself that I must make my entrance and be especially good and that then the audience would forget about their tea cups. I entered and, as it happened, the noise of tea cups ceased for several minutes – again, how fatal it is to be pleased with oneself, it is tempting the Gods! – but suddenly a noise which sounded as if at least three trays of tea had been dashed to the ground echoed round the theatre. It is true I was tired, for I was producing another play while acting in *A Month in the Country*. But I think now that it was more my vanity which was outraged. I was about to take the heroine, Natalia Petrovna, in my arms when the incident occurred. Instead of doing so I dropped her as suddenly, if more silently, than the tea trays and, turning to the audience, said with the kind of frigid authority of which among actors Mr. Noel Coward is alone the master: 'When *you* have all finished your teas, *we* will go on with the play.' I then took the alarmed and embarrassed Valerie Taylor in my arms and the play continued. The only point of this lamentable anecdote, which I need hardly say repercussed for years and has been magnified out of all proportions, was that it reduced the audience to such a cowed silence that although the play is termed a comedy no one, least of all myself, succeeded in getting another laugh during the act. As my friend Michael Shepley who was also in the cast, said to me afterwards: 'I rather admire you for having done that, but having done it, you'll never want to do it again, will you?' That was a very true and wise remark. Of course much more dreadful things have been said by actors to audiences than on that occasion. There is, I believe, the remark of George Frederick Cooke who, when playing Othello, was hissed by a Liverpool audience which must have been more versed in nineteenth-century melodrama than in Shakespeare. He stopped his performance and turned on them with fury, saying: 'So ye hiss George Frederick Cooke, do ye? Let me tell you that every stone of your damned city was cemented by the blood of a negro.' I would dearly like to have known what was the audience's reaction to that.

The best of such rebukes was caused by a slip of the tongue, when John Philip Kemble, disturbed by a squalling infant, stepped out of his part, advanced to the footlights and said:

'Ladies and gentlemen, either the play must stop or that baby cannot go on.'

It is hard to realise that it is only within the last 250 years in our theatre that the audience and the actors have come to any kind of truce. It is not only that we remember from Shakespeare's time that the groundlings were capable of understanding nothing but 'inexplicable dumb shows and noise,' but that it was not until the reign of Queen Anne, in January 1704, that a decree was passed which prevented the audience actually invading the players' domain. From the Restoration till late in the reign of Queen Anne 'politer' folks, as Cibber – or the 'quality' as Chesterfield would have called them – had been accustomed to arrogate to themselves the privilege not merely of going behind the scenes but crowding at the wings, and, at last, invading the stage itself, while the play was being acted. 'Through this mob' says Dr. Doran in his *Annals of the English Stage* 'the players had to elbow their way; and where all illusion was destroyed, difficult must have been the task, but marvellous the triumph, of those actors who could make grief appear sincere, and humour spontaneous and genuine'. This mob was not a civil and attentive crowd, but a collection of impertinent persons, who buzzed and moved about, and changed salutations with the audience or addressed the players – the chief of whom they must often have supremely exasperated. The 'decency of a clear stage' was one of Cibber's great objects, and when his importunity and the decree of Queen Anne drove the erratic part of the audience back to their proper position in the house, a change for the better was effected, by which all parties were gainers. This decree was issued in January 1704, and it prohibited 'the appearance of any of the public on the stage whatever might be their quality, the wearing of masks in any part of the house, entering the house without previous payment, and the acting of anything on the stage contrary to religion and good manners'.

We can gain some idea of the spiciness and excitement – not to say brutality – of the audiences in Betterton's time when he was first to appear in *Hamlet*. Again I cannot improve on Dr. Doran's words: 'The Jehus contend for place with the eagerness of ancient Britons in a battle of chariots. And see, the mob about the pit-doors have just caught a bailiff attempting to arrest an honest playgoer. They fasten the official up in a tub, and roll the trembling wretch all "round the square." They finish by hurling him against a carriage, which sweeps from a neighbouring street at full gallop.' At a later period we know of the story of the 'obese, little, low comedian, Hollingsworth,' who in an interval was looking at the house through an aperture in the curtain – a practice, by the way, almost superstitiously avoided in the modern English theatre – when through the aperture the twinkle of his eye was 'detected by a ruffian aloft' who, running a penknife through an apple, 'hurled it, perhaps at random, but so fatally true, that the point of the knife struck the unoffending actor so close to the eye, that for some time his sight was despaired of.'

However, it was not always the audience who took the stronger line. We are told that Peg Woffington appeared at short notice in the place of Mrs. Cibber and was advertised to play some favourite part of her own. However, she pleaded illness and would not go to the theatre. The next night, as previously advertised, she appeared as Lady Jane Grey and was greeted with a storm of hisses, provoked by her failure to appear on the evening before, when she was to have deputised for Mrs. Cibber. The audience even cried to her 'Beg pardon!' We may find excuse for the audience for wishing to chastise its favourite but we cannot help admiring Peg Woffington's courage. We are told that at that moment 'her complexion glowed with angry beauty, her eyes flashed lightning, and she walked off the stage, magnificently scornful. It was with great difficulty she was induced to return, and when she *did*, the imperious fair one calmly faced her excited audience with a "now then!" sort of look. She expressed her willingness to perform her duty, but it was for them to decide: "On or off; it must be as you please; to me it is a matter of perfect indifference!" '

All the same, the English theatre public has perhaps in the long run always been the kindest and most loyal public in the world. If, as has been said, they have less perception and enthusiasm than continental audiences, they are also not so fiercely prejudiced or partisan. They have even been accused of undue sentimentality towards their favourites. It is not an accusation that any player would wish to reproach them with. Once again, the admirable Dr. Doran provides a good example: 'The feeling of the English public towards Betterton is in strong contrast with that of the French towards their great actor, Baron. Both men grew old in the public service, but both were not treated with equal respect in the autumn of that service. Betterton, at seventy, was upheld by general esteem and crowned by general applause. When Baron, at seventy, was playing Nero, the Paris pit audience, longing for novelty, hissed him as he came down the stage. The fine old player calmly crossed his arms, and looking his rude assailants in the face, exclaimed: "Ungrateful pit! 'twas I who taught you!" That was the form of Baron's *exit*; and Clairon was as cruelly driven from the scene when her dimming eyes failed to stir the audience with the old, strange and delicious terror. In other guise did the English public part with their old friend and servant, the noble actor, fittingly described in the licence granted to him by King William, as "Thomas Betterton, Gentleman".'

It was Isaac Bickerstaff who laid it down as a rule that it was the duty of every person in the theatre audience to show his 'attention, understanding and virtue.' He might equally well have advised the players to attain the same three qualities.

It was Hamlet who advised the players to remember that there was in every audience one judicious one, the censure of which must o'erweigh a whole theatre of others. From the point of view of advice to the players, this is, to my mind, the most forcible piece of Hamlet's advice. It is also a masterly stroke of theatre, since every member of the audience, on hearing it, considers that he is that very one. There is great danger for the actor who feels that he cannot act to his best unless he knows that there is some appreciative judge 'in front.' He should remember that it takes all sorts to make an audience and that even the keenest intellect and most receptive mind cannot take in everything, but that at the same time every line of his part may well have some vivid meaning to different persons out front. He must not be like Booth – the English Barton Booth not the American Edwin – who seemed to be acting Othello very languidly one night until he surprisingly began to exert himself in the great scene of the third act, and who, when asked the cause of this sudden effort, said: 'I saw an Oxford man in the pit, for whose judgement I had more respect than for that of the rest of the audience.' He must rather believe that in every audience, whatever its size, there is most probably not only some artist or scholar or true theatregoer with a knowledge and understanding of the actor's craft who can see not only what he is achieving tonight and guess at what he intends to achieve, but also a number of people, people he will never know, who are there in order to share an experience, only too ready to be moved, whatever their inhibitions. There are those, only a few perhaps, who have never been to a theatre before, some of whom may never come again. Perhaps, also, the child who may not know what it is all about, who has never been to the theatre before, never read *Hamlet* or even heard of *The Mousetrap* but who will remember this particular night for a lifetime.

I AM NOT A CAMERA

A lecture for the Summer School of the British Film Institute at the Edinburgh Festival, Tuesday, August 24th, 1954. This is the only lecture which is not re-written for publication, beyond a few words and paragraphs to bring it a little more up to date.

SO THIS is a Summer School! Now that I can see one in the flesh and blood the mental picture I had made of a Summer School has already begun to fade. Of course I cannot see you very well, standing up here on the stage of a darkened cinema, that spotlight in my eyes – but the bright, sunny slopes of a green campus, with golden lads and lasses in blue jeans and bright cotton dresses, with here and there a bearded and perhaps kilted sage ... whither are they fled? Ah, well! ... In any case all I felt I could be certain of was that the audience of a Summer School would know why it had assembled, and that no one here this morning – as can only too easily happen at all points of this city at all hours of the day during this yearly Saturnalia of the Athens of the North – no one here this morning would be confidently expecting the performance of a Schubert song-cycle or an illustrated recital of lesser-known folk dances. You are all awaiting, I am sure, since we are under the auspices of the British Film Institute, a more or less authoritative lecture on Film. I regret to inform you that you are mistaken.

In spite of my nearly twenty years in the film industry I

have no doubt that many of you could give a far more searching analysis of Film in all its comical-historical-pastoral-topical-technical-ethnological-and-psychological aspects than I could set forth in a month of temperance Sundays. For I am primarily a stage actor, and though I have on several occasions been numbered among those mysterious elect known as the 'Box-Office Ten,' my aversion to being referred to as 'the Film Star' amounts to nausea and I have as resolutely refused to have my portrait in bold bad Technicolor on the stairways of the local Odeons and Gaumonts as I have, politely I hope, declined to let anyone start a fan club for me. Nevertheless I accept up to a point the proposition that no actor can be an entirely private person and I am amiable, within the bounds of decorum, towards 'fans' until, as occasionally happens, they become uncivil, or accost me warmly by the wrong name. Mr. Wilding and Mr. Rennie must, I am sure, share my feelings. I am considerably more patient and polite to columnists than some of them are to actors.

So you see you must not expect very much. I will not insult you by giving you a rehash of Pudovkin on Film Acting – a good book provided that you are not a dialectical materialist – nor of Grierson on Documentary. I will try to avoid all reference to the Film Critics. Nevertheless, despite the fact that I so definitely am not a Camera and am much too wrapped up in my own processes of creation to observe at all accurately what has been going on under my nose in these past twenty years, a few diffused impressions have remained and such as they are – largely autobiographical and entirely eclectic – I propose to try to bring them into focus.

I went into films against what I thought was my better judgment. This is understandable, I think, if you can remember that, in 1938, British films, with certain honourable exceptions, were a joke scarcely worth making. I did not, I hasten to explain, despise films as films. I had been addicted to them since the days when I was taken to see Miss Annette Kellerman, the aquatic actress, emoting under water in a stuffy Bioscope which had formerly been Terry's Theatre in the Strand (now Woolworths). I saw *Intolerance* (at the Stoll Opera House in Kingsway) and walked home with my mother while the searchlights picked out the German aircraft, which somehow seemed much less real than Griffith's masterpiece. *The Rink*, *The Tramp*, *Shoulder Arms*, *The Kid* and much later the early Garbo pictures – all these and many others I saw and loved.

As an undergraduate film critic on *The Granta* I solemnly predicted that talkies would never last, or, if they did, that they would be the ruin of the cinema. There are those who think that on this point I have yet to be proved wrong but that was only one of the many rash verdicts I pronounced from the comfortable cathedra of a free seat at the flicks. It was about this time I came into contact with two of my friends, Humphrey Jennings and Basil Wright. I remember vividly certain scenes of what must have been Wright's first film, which he shot himself – with I suppose some help, for he also was the protagonist – in sixteen millimetre. It was a naïve little story of a young fellow from the country who came up to town for the day and got so confused by the London traffic and the noise and all the rest of it that he lost his nerve, his reason – represented by a taut string which broke – and finally his life, knocked down by a motor vehicle of some sort – a bus, I fancy – somewhere near Hyde Park Corner. I wish this piece of juvenilia still existed. I remember the general impression vividly and it had some of the lyrical touches which distinguish some of Wright's mature work, as in *The Song of Ceylon*. It was exactly cut, I think, to the music, which was Arthur Bliss's *Rout* played on a 'table-grand.'

Around the corner from Wright's rooms the Cambridge Union Film Society showed us some of the great Russian silent classics and I think I saw most of these. I remember an especial fondness for *Turk-Sib* – a documentary about the creation of the Turkestan-Siberian railway, with its remarkable shots of the irrigation of the desert and the steady push forward of the iron way across the barren wastes. Before this, as a student in Heidelberg, I saw, several times, *The Student of Prague*, *The Golem*, the Fritz Lang *Nibelung* Saga and the early silent films of the demonic, elegant Conrad Veidt and the astonishing and unforgettable young Bergner.

So that, with all this, it seems to me a little odd that when at last I became an actor I should have made such a shy and crab-like approach to film acting.

The fact is that I was a snob. Not because I had been suckled on continental silent 'classics,' for I was equally avid to see the *Ben Hurs*, the *Big Parades*, the Clara Bows, the early Joan Crawfords – how splendid it is that she can still outstare us all! – but because I had become a stage actor, and in the thirties, few serious actors of the English stage except Charles Laughton took the English movies seriously. As Ralph Richardson wrote to me when I told him that I was offered a film contract: 'Films are where you sell what you have learnt on the stage.' That is not quite true, but, all the same, there is some truth in it.

The majority of young actors and actresses start out with only the vaguest, most romantic notions of their goal. Stardom, names in lights, bowing to a crowded theatre, seeing heads turn to stare in the street: the same heady mixture which has intoxicated generation after generation. Relatively few have any idea of what kind of actor they want to be. It is not easy to shape a career in the theatre, but it can be done. It is almost impossible for the actor to shape one in the English cinema (or to shape one *for himself, by himself,* anywhere). At this moment, though we have many very popular and successful actors, and leaving aside as an exception Olivier's Shakespeare films, there would seem to be only one English actor who has as it were imposed his manner and style on his films and that, of course, is Alec Guinness. Nevertheless there is a great deal more intelligent, imaginative, and creative as opposed to imitative film-making going on now than in the thirties. In 1938 in England, with the exceptions of Hitchcock, the much under-rated Will Hay comedies and a few documentaries, the Korda historical romances and his *Shape of Things to Come,* there just seemed to be an eddying current of films – some of them shot with little or no script – in which the actor could sink or swim, swim if he were lucky and if that was what he wanted, across the Atlantic on a Hollywood contract with one-sided options. So that, supported by my friends, my idols of the British Theatre, most of whom only did occasional films, some none at all, I held back from film-acting, for I could see that what one of them said was partly true: 'You only have to stand up straight and be able to talk the King's English for someone to *offer* you a film contract.' I remembered the advice from, oddly enough, a Hollywood director, George Cukor – a very shrewd observer: 'Don't go into films, kid, until they go on their knees to you.'

This advice and these persuasions I followed. I refused film tests – which only intrigued the producers more and caused my agent some embarrassment. I tried to explain to him that Edith Evans had done no film, Peggy Ashcroft only one or two, and that Gielgud's attempts had not enhanced his great reputation. I told him that I couldn't learn to act by making films.

I would give the same advice to any young actor or actress today. This may sound not a little smug. But it is all the same true that there are some dizzy dozens of film names who discover, too late, that the technique of screen acting is largely a matter of selection and that having no range of acting resources they have little from which to select. They then repeat the same performance which, according to their health, looks and vigour, satisfies the public until on a certain date, after a certain not so successful film or films, and by the sortilege of fashion, they have to find something else to do.

I received a letter the other day (1958) which touches on this, from a young actor whom I had recommended to a repertory company and, some years later, to the casting director of a film company. He writes from Hollywood, where he now receives star-billing, asking for 'more advice.'

'The work I have done, although maybe bad, has taught me a lot. But the more I learn the less I seem to know and the more I want to do good work. Suddenly I'm glad I'm young because there is so much to do and such a short time in which to do it. I am impatient (with enthusiasm of youth) for satisfaction yet I do not wish to shorten the growth of the ultimate result . . . I sometimes become frightened that in this quest for knowledge I will miss some human movement or lose the objective of the continual search with the blindness of searching.'

On the other hand there are those, like Chaplin or Garbo or some dozen names – not more – that you may care to suggest, who have done more or less the same things in more or less exactly the same way through decades and who are nevertheless the great names of the cinema. How do we account for this?

In the case of the Clara Bows, the Carole Lombards, the Valentinos, we may add to their somewhat limited talents the potent, immediate pull of their remarkable looks, plus their correspondence to some contemporary taste. I think we should also notice, as in the early films of Mary Pickford or Douglas Fairbanks, that even when we view them now their performances are altogether more persuasive than those of the surrounding casts.

To do the same thing over and over again would seem to be an easy task. To do it over years and years and keep a world public fascinated by the spectacle is not so easy. That requires, if not genius, something more than talent. Valentino was not only a face and a fashion. He had an instinctively fastidious technique and knew what to hold back.

Leslie Henson once told me a story about Chaplin which, if it is not true, I still believe. With it should be remembered the now famous story of how he created his famous tramp character by being sent at short notice into the dressing room on the Californian beach where some of the earliest of his silent films were shot – films in which he did not star – and where he picked out someone's trousers, another actor's boots, a hat and cane from goodness knows where, stuck on half a slap-stick comedian's moustache and waddled onto the beach in the manner of Fred Karno. From which indebted impromptu, it is said, the Chaplin tramp was born. But Henson's other story seems to me more fascinating, typical and true. It is this. A famous 'gag' writer – someone, let us suppose, who worked for the Marx Brothers – was recently allowed to visit Chaplin's set while he was rehearsing a scene. Moved and excited at the end of the rehearsal the 'gag' man ventured to speak to Chaplin and said, after the compliments and thanks were over, that he had an idea, an idea which if Mr. Chaplin liked, he would be pleased to present to the great comedian free, gratis and for nothing, for it would be an honour. Chaplin listened, it is said, and remarked that the new gag, the new twist, the 'pay-off,' or whatever it was, was a good idea, a very good idea indeed. His visitor repeated his offer of it as a gift. He would be proud if Mr. Chaplin used it. The comedian replied that, truly excellent as the idea was, he would not be using it.

'But Mr. Chaplin, why not?'

'Because it's never been done before.'

Embedded in these two stories is an idea as old as the sun. For like the sun and the moon, the old ideas go on. It is only the not inconsiderable question of doing them differently each day, and from time to time better than anyone remembers them being done before. An actor may achieve many things by practice and experience but originality is not one of them.

We live in an age where more entertainment is offered per person per square mile than has ever been available before. Whether as actors or directors or writers, we are working for a public which has been made particularly alive to all the tricks and gimmicks of the showman and the artist. I choose to put it that way rather than to say it is a more critical public. In my boyhood I regarded Theda Bara or Gloria Swanson simply as phenomena, stars whose brightness one did not question, one just blinked at them. Nowadays I imagine any bright schoolboy could give a shrewd analysis of what even schoolboys call the Marilyn Monroe doctrine.

In this highly, artificially charged atmosphere actors must continually create the illusion that they are doing something new or at least something spontaneous. But it is important to remember that there is nothing that is really new. The originality lies in 'how'; not in 'what.' The discovery that there were only thirty-six dramatic situations in all dramatic literature, which was made by Gozzi over two hundred years ago, is still true today, however hard critics and dramatists have tried to disprove it. And these dramatic situations also cover every kind of film which contains a story involving human beings. Only those films which are strictly documentary or which have no dramatic content at all manage to evade being catalogued in this mystic number. This is just as well for the actor. Since the world does not seem to have tired of those thirty-six possibilities – with, of course, the interbreeding of two or more of them – the actor seems still likely to be able to earn his living until the remote day when people cease to be interested in 'fiction' and are prepared to contemplate only the 'factual.' I am glad that I shall not be there for that cold, clear dawn.

* * *

Let me go back to the beginnings of my first acquaintance with the Melpomene of the silver screen and her attendant bitch goddess. Having at last, in 1938, succumbed to the blandishments of Gainsborough Pictures (1928) Limited, I found from reading my papers that I was to be 'teamed' with a very popular actress who has since been described on occasions as 'the first lady of our screen.' This was somewhat alarming to both the lady and myself. We were first introduced at a Charity Film Ball in the Royal Albert Hall where we danced together and were photographed in a tight embrace which would suggest that, to say the least, we knew each other quite well. My first day's work consisted of a scene which was designed to show how boy meets girl and, as everybody who has ever seen films knows, boy must meet girl in a way that is unusual and, if

In the ruins of Angkor on a visit to Cambodia during the filming of the location scenes of *The Quiet American*, 1957.

JOHN WORTHING in *The Importance of being Earnest*: directed by Anthony Asquith, 1952.

Left, ANDREW CROCKER-HARRIS in *The Browning Version*: directed by Anthony Asquith, 1951. *Right*, DÉLIOT in *The Green Scarf*: directed by George More O'Farrell, 1954.

possible, cute. The girl, a rich heiress stranded in a middle-European hotel, was arrogant enough to persuade the manager to turn the young man out of the room above because he, a student of folk music, and his companions were making far too much noise dancing in their room upstairs. The young man is evicted from his room and in revenge makes his way into that of the girl, announcing, with a degree of arrogance and bad taste which certainly caps hers, that he is going to spend the night in her room. This beginning to my partnership with Margaret Lockwood, whom, as I've explained, I scarcely knew, may seem an amusing introduction. All the same it was not the ideal one for either of us. In the first place I immediately sensed the loss of that essential to good acting on the stage, the rapport between artists who have worked together for at least the rehearsal period. This is, from the actor's point of view, probably the gravest disadvantage of acting for the camera, for one is continually having to play important scenes with other actors with whom one has never played, possibly never even met. These scenes can sometimes be shot in a morning after a hurried introduction and there they are, inexorably, in the printed film. Often the other actor has not been given the advantage of reading the full script.

The next thing I found I had to learn in my first film was rather surprising to me, for I would have expected the very opposite. It is generally supposed that acting for the stage involves a number of artificial gestures and movements which the actors would not conceivably use in ordinary life. That is not quite so. In the theatre it is not only possible but essential for the actor to find a sequence of physical movements which –allowing for certain conventions such as raising the voice when playing up-stage – seems completely natural to him.

Indeed, a break in the flow of his physical movements can disturb or even destroy the stage actor's sense of inner reality. A good director and good actors can so arrange the movement that the characters do not mask each other or make disturbing movements during each other's lines, and yet individually feel that each is in his right place. It is not at all the same in front of the camera, where one is frequently obliged to stand much closer to one's partner than one would ever do in ordinary life, or balance one's voice to a more even level because the microphone cannot 'take' extreme changes of volume.

I was prepared, to some extent, for the rigid pattern imposed by the camera movement. What I was not prepared for was to find that I had to 'cheat' my movements and that the camera by being able to point in any direction does to some extent upset the audience's judgment of where things are when seen from a different angle, so that at each 'cut', actors, furniture and even the set are subject to a series of 'cheats.'

Indeed the elaborate realism of a big film set is for the actor only persuasive at the first rehearsal of the first shot on that set, when it is unlit but, after all, complete. From that moment on, the set disintegrates until finally it is, probably, a mere corner, brightly lit in a forest of lamps and lighting apparatus. It is often difficult to get onto what remains of the set at all. It is hard for the actor, when he begins making films, to understand that whereas in one shot he, say, entered a room and could see another character waiting for him in a certain spot, he may be required to look somewhere else when the two characters come face to face in another shot.

I understand all that now, of course, and have adapted myself to it. But to this day I find on occasion that the inflexibility of the cinema, which demands, for example, that if you have sat down on a certain word of a sentence you should sit down on precisely the same word in another take or from another angle, can produce a wooden effect. It will inhibit the actor until such time as, when he has done enough films, he has developed a technique of doing all those tricky little things such as hitting chalk marks, adjusting his gaze to just right or left of the lens and all the rest of the complicated artifice of film-making to the point where they become second nature. For, contrary to what you might expect one who is primarily a stage actor to say, I believe that in good acting there is a continual flow of improvisation, a little tributary stream to freshen, as it were, the main current in its set course.

In the early rehearsals of a stage play or a film the actor is to a large extent improvising, however carefully he may have studied the words and meaning of his part. These improvisations then have to be swiftly selected and notated until they are no longer strictly speaking improvised. But within this notated framework there must be a quality of the moment, an imaginative freshness each time the scene is played so that the actor feels that he is saying those very words or doing those very things for the very first time, every time. If I say that even the finest actors and actresses of the stage will admit that it is only from time to time that they satisfy themselves in this matter throughout a long stage rôle, how much more easy is it to understand that the film actor, conceiving and developing and constructing a long part over many months, usually out of continuity, jig-saw fashion, very seldom satisfies himself throughout even one morning – there is always some line, some move, some look, some little hesitation he feels he might have done better. Here he is often wrong. Occasionally perhaps, when we see a scene as finally 'cut,' we realise that extra emphasis here, or a lesser emphasis there, would have made it neater and clearer. But it is a common fault of film acting that we tend to suppose we must be expressing something or other through every foot of film. The actor can never be wholly unconscious of the effects he is making, but frequently his most telling moments are those when, as in life, he does nothing very much or reacts in exactly the opposite way to what we might expect.

Frequently certain moments of early 'takes' are altogether more plausible and effective than when, after repeated 'takes,' the actor has begun to 'set' his performance. As he begins to do this, consciously to polish little moments which grew out of improvisation, he tends to lose that first impetus which gave life to the scene. He sometimes begins to forget the situation, or to anticipate a climax. This anticipation of a climax is one of the commonest traps of the actor, either on the stage or screen. It is easier to avoid this pitfall on the screen, for the actor is not conscious of how the climax of the scene will shape – whereas on the stage the actor has heard it all through rehearsals and night after night.

This is all to do with that creative mood which must be found before real acting can begin. When it is found nothing seems an effort. Unless it is found everything is. Fortunately for actors who love acting with all their heart and soul and who do not secretly despise their craft this mood is at hand more or less at will.

* * *

I have learned nearly all of the little I know about film through my directors. From Hitchcock who directed my first film I learned to do as I was told and not to worry too much. Hitchcock, being the brilliant master of the technical side of his script that he is, knew that he could get a performance out of me by his own skill in cutting. He knew that mine was a very good part, that I was more or less the right type for it, that I was sufficiently trained to be able to rattle off my lines and that mercifully, since I was aware that not even the cleverest cameraman in the world could make me look like Robert Taylor, I was never particularly camera-conscious. But he also sensed that I thought the whole atmosphere of filming was, to say the least, uncongenial compared to that obtaining in the theatre where every night I was playing in a Chehov play with John Gielgud, Peggy Ashcroft, Gwen Ffrangçon-Davies, Alec Guinness and a completely remarkable cast. One of Hitchcock's tricks which he works on the psychology of the public is to cast actors against their type, a trick he has managed often with great success; he also uses shock tactics on actors and besides his famous practical jokes he likes to 'rib' his actors, believing, sometimes but not always correctly, that actors, who have an infinite capacity for taking praise, are jogged into a more awake state if humorously insulted. I well remember him saying 'Actors are cattle!' I can see now that he was trying to jolt me out of my unrealistic dislike of working conditions in the studios and what he thought was a romantic reverence for the theatre. *The Lady Vanishes* is considered by many people as vintage Hitchcock. I could never bring myself to see it until fifteen years later, in New York, where it is still frequently shown.

The method of my second director, Paul Czinner, was in most ways the complete reverse. He overwhelmed me with subtle praise in order to make me feel that I was a good enough actor to play opposite my adored Elisabeth Bergner. He further explained to me that whereas there was never time for what stage actors would call proper rehearsals, the camera was often able to catch the artist's emotions or reactions when these were still in their early, improvisatory stages. He printed all the takes, and there were usually a great many, of all the shots. 'Rushes' each day frequently ran for threequarters of an hour or more. He explained that by frequent close cutting and the selection of a look from one take, a line from another and a particular though perhaps quite irrelevant expression from the third, a performance was often very much richer than the actor felt it to be even in his 'best' take. He personally directed the editing of the film over many months, and no editing was begun until the shooting of the film was completed.

This of course is a very expensive method and has gone completely out of fashion. The tendency now is to use less 'cross-cutting' and a great number of tracking shots, and much work is done from 'dollies' and cranes. In a way this would seem to be preferable from the actor's point of view for it allows him to build up a scene, to know how he is going to make his effects more or less on his own. But some of these moving shots are extremely tricky for the technicians as well as for the actor and it is very galling for the actor to find that the take which he has felt to be unquestionably the best from the acting point of view has to be scrapped because someone fancies he could see a mike shadow. After a time the actor learns to be philosophical about this and to realise that it puts a further onus on him to be as good as he can be all the time. Nevertheless only very few actors can afford half way through a take which they know is not to their liking deliberately to 'dry' and compel the scene to be started again. Filming is, after all, an enormously expensive business and there are always too many film actors out of work. However, if it is permitted for the cameraman or the sound department to reject takes or whole scenes because they are not personally satisfied with the technical result, it should also be permitted to the actor to veto certain takes. The usual objection to this is that actors only look at themselves in the rushes anyway, and are quite incapable of judging the scene as a whole. There is some truth in that but in my opinion each department of the film industry does exactly the same thing and only concentrates on its own work. A mike shadow or a camera wobble seldom really disturb the public in a good scene.

* * *

It was perhaps from Carol Reed, with whom I made my third film and with whom I was to make two more that I learned for the first time how intimate the relationship between actor and film director can be. Reed understands the actor's temperament perhaps as well as any director alive. The theatre and acting are in his blood and he is able, with infinite pains and care, to give the actor the feeling that everything is up to him and that all the director is doing is to make sure that he is being seen to his best advantage. A very warm and friendly feeling prevails, not only on the set, and the actor is encouraged to feel that he has also assisted in the preparation of the film. Indeed Reed frequently did ask my opinions and I think on several occasions adopted suggestions of mine. Such as when we were shooting *The Stars Look Down* in a narrow street of miners' cottages in Cumberland and I noticed a child sweeping up a puddle in the road with a determination in its face and a sensuous pleasure in every sweep of the broom. I do not remember now whether this decorative incident is in the finished film, for by the time the camera had to turn the child's mother had dressed her in her Sunday frock and put her hair in ribbons. I do remember Reed being infinitely tactful about this. He is enormously considerate of other people's feelings but underneath this gentle velvet glove is an iron will which eleven times out of ten will have its own way in the end. I find this entirely admirable.

Reed is one of those dedicated beings, the artist who is completely absorbed by his dream. He eats, drinks and sleeps cinema. You might hear him carrying on an eager conversation with a farmer, a chemist or a nuclear physicist but that would not mean he is even for a moment interested in farming, chemistry or nuclear physics. It would be more likely that he was studying the farmer's way of scratching his head to punctuate his conversation, the chemist's tone of voice or the particular physicist's calm way of letting drop horrendous statistics. He would not be purposely observing these. It is his habit. If he had nothing else to observe he would watch a flea. He has a very friendly and charming way of asking a lot of gentle questions and watching you as you give the answers with his big blue eyes as wide as a child's when listening to a story. The wide ingenuousness is almost too good to be true and his repeated exclamations of surprise or incredulity: 'Do you really?' 'That's fascinating!' 'How true!' would strike one as naïve to the point of absurdity if after a short time one did not become aware that these simple, direct questions are not so simple nor so direct as they seem. Unwittingly you have supplied him with an answer or clue to some quite different question. He would, I think, disclaim this and he seldom, I am sure, consciously lays traps. He is not an intellectual man and like most intuitive artists he mistrusts analysis. He is not startlingly original, nor particularly daring. Being schooled in the hard school of commercial cinema under such experts as the late Ted Black, and of success by his early master, Edgar Wallace, one of his big blue eyes always has at least an oblique squint in the direction of the box office. This,

I would have you understand, is not intended as criticism of Reed's achievement. Some of the greatest and most daringly original artists are often considerable showmen. One has only to think of Picasso. And sometimes the best originality is the originality that conceals itself. Our commercial cinema which, to do it justice, is not so slow to take up and use bright new talents as some may think, either destroys them, swiftly rejects them or forces them to conform. An original cinema artist would prefer after all to conform to some extent and make films rather than cease to make films at all, though there are exceptions, such as von Stroheim. The tyranny of the 'boys in the front office' so brilliantly reported by Lillian Ross in her book *Picture* about the making and massacre of John Huston's *Red Badge of Courage* should be compulsory reading for armchair critics who do not realise that 'Art Cinema' is to some degree even in such countries as France and Italy, and to a much greater degree in the English-speaking countries, ineluctably geared to the statistics of the box-office and the distributing circuits.

This is the inherent and inevitable trap of dealing in a medium which is economically expensive. Korda once said to me: 'No actor is worth all the money your agent is asking.' My reply was that for that matter no film is intrinsically worth its cost. The cost and the ever increasing cost of film-making touches every member of the film industry. It has driven writers and directors to the streets and the open air where most of the true poetry of the cinema has been found. That has been good. But the cost of the box-office and the exhibitors' fondness for a 'predigested' diet have banished a brilliant, original mind like that of Cavalcanti back to his native Brazil, and they have hung round the neck of Orson Welles his own wanderlust till it has become a millstone.

Cavalcanti I miss most bitterly not only for the little we did together but for the much we planned to do.* In the 'Ventriloquist' sequence in *Dead of Night* we both felt that it was impossible to tell where direction or acting ended or began. This is, I must stress, ideal not only from the actor's point of view, but from every point of view. Ideally, there should be no line of demarcation between writer, actor and director, and the camera-man should be as sensitive to this phenomenon as his negative is to light and shadow. It is worth noting, in passing, that nearly all the best cameramen have this gentle, hypersensitive but co-operative and dependable nature.

This creative collaboration I have in varying degrees experienced a number of times and when it happens film-making becomes every bit as absorbing and exciting for the actor as the creation of a great rôle on the stage. There have been occasions, as when working with Orson Welles, even till 3.30 in the morning, when I have not wanted to stop. I had it also with Asquith, several times, especially in *The Browning Version*. With Reed again in *Kipps*, when we worked at Shepherds Bush throughout the 1940 blitz, when we were both living in flats in the same building, so that we could meet in the evenings and talk; a time I remember above all because of its utter divorce from any reality except that of imaginative work. For to face the cameras each morning as a younger man than myself I was obliged to take heavy sleeping pills each night in order to sleep through the noise of the bombardment. No question then of retiring to a shelter. And there in the morning on the set would be Diana Wynyard, who often had to drive through the tail-end of the raid to have her hair washed and set and be made up and ready to appear by 8 o'clock, ravishingly gowned by Cecil Beaton and only a degree less beautiful then than she is now,

* Cavalcanti is now working again in Europe.

several years later. In the evenings we left the studio ten minutes before blackout and as we drove home in the dusk the sirens would start. If they did not, I remember, we were faintly worried. No wonder that my memory of the blitz is largely a picture of a fictitious Folkestone in Edwardian dress.

I could ramble on at length about working with different types of director. I could tell you of working with Fritz Lang – one of the great names of the cinema, surely – who taught me what it is like to be caught up in the Hollywood machine, working in a studio where your personal telephone calls are liable to be tapped. Lang would often ask me about working in England. It seemed to be the dream of most of the lively creative talents in Hollywood and New York in 1947. I urged him to come and direct Dylan Thomas' *The Doctor and the Devils*, which I had persuaded the Rank Organisation to buy for me – for Lang had shown by his first film for M.G.M., *Fury*, that he, like Renoir in his *Swamp Water* and *The Southerner*, could triumphantly absorb material which was not native to him. *The Doctor and the Devils*, which Dylan Thomas later published in script form, was one of many subjects I tried hard to get made about that time. I was told it was impossible because a 'B' picture with, I think, Boris Karloff, on the subject of the body-snatchers, had been made a year or two before.

The film I made in Hollywood with Lang – and which, by the way, I have never seen – had a silly story, pseudo-psychological and pretentious, but as Lang had just made two very successful and exciting pictures out of stories which seemed to me equally preposterous, I accepted it. I wanted to work with Lang. I thought I could learn something from him. I certainly learnt one thing, even if I did not know it already: that in ninety-nine cases out of a hundred, the creative germ of a picture is in its idea. With a good germinating idea and with the help of a good script, you have the best chance of making a good picture. I have often found, when people have asked me what my new picture is about, that if I can give them an answer in one or two sentences: 'It's about a ventriloquist who is obsessed by the idea that his dummy controls him'; 'It's about an elderly, embittered schoolmaster whose defences break down because someone is kind to him'; 'It's about an unsuccessful barrister who is given an almost impossible case, which nobody else will touch, and who wins it,' etc., their swift reaction of interest is a fair indication, if not a final one, of the film's popular appeal. Not all good pictures are subject to this reduction, but if you have a germinating idea, an idea which not only catches the imagination of the public, but which fires the minds of the writer, the director, the actors and everyone working on the picture, you are half-way there. Best of all, as I have heard Welles say, is to believe that each film you make will be a *great* picture. 'If you don't believe it will be *great* there's little chance of it being anything but just another picture.' He is right. And it is something one must believe, not just something one says.

Joseph L. Mankiewicz is a man who believes that. Here is one of the most talented men I have ever worked with. In common with all the finest directors he has, of course, the prerequisite: the gift of being able to tell his story through the lens. To this one may add scholarship and a wide erudition, a piercing judgment of character, and an intelligence which takes him swiftly to the heart of the matter. He has the curiosity of Reed, the culture of Asquith, the apparently inexhaustible vitality of Gene Kelly—with whom I worked in Paris on *The Happy Road* and was seldom happier. Mankiewicz also has the on the whole enviable, American quality of making life seem as if it were happening as he has ordered it to happen. When it does not, even his considerable patience has a hint of thunder in it. As a script-writer I would say he has few equals, as a producer the drive of a large locomotive, as a director he gets what he wants. Since he sometimes combines all three of these functions, as he did in *The Quiet American*, it is a good thing that he does not wish to be an actor as well.

Not only is he not an actor but he never could have been, for anyone with such positive beliefs and forceful opinions must be the least suggestible of men. An actor is nothing if not suggestible.

Mankiewicz never praises, except inadvertently or by implication. When an actor would occasionally ask, after a final take, if it was 'really all right' he would answer: 'I wouldn't print it if it wasn't.' I liked this myself, having formed a very high opinion of his critical faculties, but I noticed that he seldom tried to get more out of some actors than could be seen to be there and I wonder, knowing how insecure most actors can feel, whether an occasional pat on the back might not have produced something which would have surprised him. But there is no knowing whether he may not have done this by another method which is the most stimulating of all: to receive praise through a third person.

What is certain in this matter is that no praise at all can be as harmful as extravagant or faint praise if the actor thinks the director doesn't really care.

The trouble is, of course, that there are never enough germinating ideas around every week of the year to supply films that will fill all those thousands of cinemas, let alone the ravening maw of television. The director or the actor will be forced to accept ideas which do not immediately hit the jackpot of his imagination. There are many good ideas which seem intractable at first.

There are dozens of films which have been lifted out of the ordinary by men of talent. There is that script lying there on my table; why should that not be just such another? There are good germinating ideas which tumble into the wrong heads; a *trouvaille* of Henry James, who should have written *The Spanish Gardener*. There is also the rent to pay, or the children's school bills.

* * *

The singleness of purpose of men like Flaherty is rare. The universal genius of a Chaplin is rarer still. The writer, the director, the actor must work, not only because of the rent, but because quite simply their health and happiness depend on some form of creation. And always there is the inexorable, baleful axiom which even the greatest must face: that the best is the enemy of the good. To take a recent instance, one or two critics took pains to observe that Reed's *Outcast of the Islands*, which apparently disappointed many, would have been hailed heartily had it been the work of an unknown. Environment and circumstances play a large and often unpredictable part in general taste. You are certain, for instance, to judge some films which you will see at this Festival quite differently than if you were to see them at your local cinema. We seldom realise what chance influences can affect us deeply as members of an audience. There is the rueful pleasure in finding something much more to our taste than critical opinion has led us to expect. There is the perverse pleasure, not untinged with envy, in reversing general acclaim. Part of our critical make-up, if we pride ourselves on being critical, is to be able to grieve with the judicious. But I think we sometimes grieve a little ostentatiously and do not make due allowance for the shifting no-man's-land of what 'comes off.' It comes off for some and not for others. When it comes off for you its imperfections fade, when it does not they loom large.

What about the prejudices which attend every successful career? For show me a talent about whom there is not controversy and I will show you a dull talent. How does one account for the reception of Renoir's *Swamp Water* (renamed *The Man who Lost Himself* and which ran for one week at the London Pavilion)? It was generally stated that all European directors lose their talent in Hollywood and that Renoir had lost his. Yet *Swamp Water* was, directorially, every bit as good as Renoir's next American picture *The Southerner*. The latter picture had a more popular idea, but *Swamp Water*, as picture making, was to my mind equally good and perhaps in some points better. Why do critics of a film made from a novel tend, even if it is a good film, to like it if they have not read the novel and dislike it if they have? We must grant they have some reason here sometimes. But not always. The film writer and director have told the same story in their different fashions just as two different novelists might have told it in theirs. The mixed reception of the recent *Father Brown* was a case in point. Why does a film made from a play automatically expose itself to critical broadsides? Is there so much *inherent* difference in a story suitable for the stage and one suitable for the screen? Often, but not always. I remember the enthusiastic reception of a little French trifle, Becker's *Edouard et Caroline*. The credit titles certainly acknowledged no playwright and for all I know *Edouard et Caroline* was never a play. But can we be sure that at one time, even if only in the author's mind, it was not? For this charming little picture was, if you remember, in complete three act form and much of its appeal lay in its happy dialogue. The first act was in the garret where the hero and heroine lived, the second in the big house where the party took place, the third in the garret again. Becker hardly ever showed us the exteriors of these; they were not germane to the story which was a simple idea of a quarrel between two young people in love. It is not necessary to keep moving from set to set to achieve cinematic movement – as the old silent classic *Bett und Sofa* demonstrated. *Edouard et Caroline* was no more Pure Film than the transcriptions of *Quiet Weekend* and *Quiet Wedding*. It had a little more unity, perhaps, and was rather better acted.

* * *

Finally, and to get back to my main theme, what about the current fashionable prejudice about the superiority of the non-actor, the well-directed amateur, to the trained professional? Despite early pictures such as *The Cabinet of Dr. Caligari*, the *Nibelungs*, the Cartoons of Disney, the Shakespeare films of Olivier, a tendency towards realism has always been the trademark of films. No wonder that there should have grown up an increasing interest in what are known as real people. How understandable, and what a fallacy! For, except in the materialistic sense, Madame Bovary is much more real to us than any lady now present in this cinema. If you do not know him already, you all have the chance of knowing more about Pickwick or Raskolnikov than you will ever know about me, or I about you.

After a long tracking-shot of a line of actors on parade for a prison-camp scene, the director thought he would have a complementary shot of some of the soldiers who were lent to the film company as extras. 'Now let's have some *real* faces' he exclaimed. And in a recent issue of *Sight and Sound* a critic of the Franco-English film *Knave of Hearts* also delights in the fact that the hidden camera in the streets gives us 'real' faces. In the sense that the average film extra's face is not real, since self-conscious-

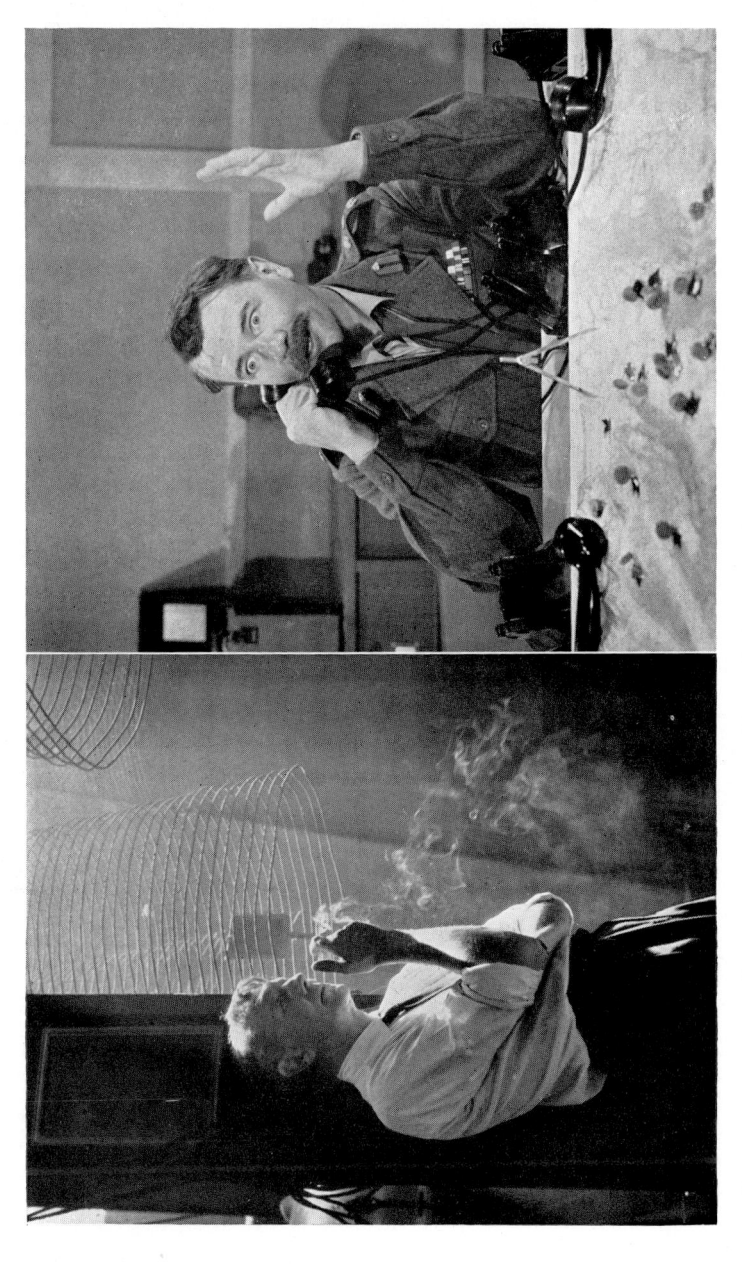

Left, Fowler in *The Quiet American*: directed by Joseph L. Mankiewicz, 1957. *Right*, General Medworth in *The Happy Road*: directed by Gene Kelly, 1957.

Right, Sir Arthur in *Behind the Mask*: directed by Brian Desmond Hurst, 1957. *Below*, The Confidence Trickster in *Law and Disorder*: directed by Charles Crichton, 1957.

ness makes his face temporarily not his own, I share this delight. Film-extras are not highly skilled or they would not be film-extras. But the face of Spencer Tracy? Is that not real? Even when, as occasionally, he will 'mug' to get a laugh, for in private life do not we all occasionally 'mug' to show our feelings or underline a point? This prejudice is easily understood. It is not that Spencer Tracy's face, or my face for that matter, is less real than that of a postman or some R.A.F. Pilot, it is that over the years, after seeing an actor play a number of different rôles, there is an accretion of past association, multiple, complex beyond analysis. If the actor is of a lively imagination, as all good actors are, he soon secures that suspension of disbelief which is to my mind the indispensable stepping-stone to a work of art. Without such an actor and such suspension of disbelief, *Monsieur Vincent*, the film of the life of St. Vincent de Paul, would never have moved us as it did. I have not seen the film of Eliot's *Murder in the Cathedral* but I have been given every reason to doubt that the priest who played Thomas à Becket could persuade us as Pierre Fresnay persuaded us. Persuasion is what matters in art, not conviction.

When Guinness or Danny Kaye plays six different parts in one film, what do we feel then? Oh, that is different, we say, for that is a *tour de force* which demands our suspension of disbelief. If Guinness or Paul Muni, or one or two other actors, disguise themselves utterly, what then? Again we accept this if it comes off. If it comes off rarely in films it is because it is comparatively rarely attempted, owing to the expense of the medium. To create a complete character performance can only be trusted to established actors who are masters of that branch of acting whereby actors change visibly from part to part, even to the point of putting on weight or taking it off at will. This is not necessarily the highest branch of the acting art but it is not an easy one to climb.

It is a problem I have had several times in films, notably in *The Browning Version* and *The Dam Busters*. For both of these we had several make-up tests which were also sound tests, so that I could hear how I was sounding, for when one first assumes a voice or an accent it sounds in one's own head very exaggerated. In the second of these films I was called on to impersonate a living character, Barnes Wallis. I spent a few hours with him on various occasions. But on the second day of meeting him I said 'I am not going to mimic you, you know.' His reply was interesting, not because of his evident relief, but because it illustrated so well the scientist's mind, always eager to tackle a problem, even in a field of acting. He remarked, after a few seconds' pause, 'No, of course not, your problem is not to imitate a person but to create one.'

Nor is it easy, of course, to take a child and mould a performance out of him such as Reed did in *The Fallen Idol*, or as de Sica did with the hero of *Bicycle Thieves*, or as Pudovkin claims can be done with anyone, more or less, by the director's art. By the way, which of you, with your hand on your heart, could swear, if you did not know the name of Aldo Fabrizi, which of the actors in *Bicycle Thieves* was a professional actor?

It will have been seen, I hope, that I have no wish to be dogmatic and I must step warily to my conclusion, which I believe to be none the less true if it is shadowed by a question mark. The right questions, to my mind, are more valuable than answers, and nearly always more permanent.

I have made it clear, I hope, that I accept and admire the scope of documentary film making. I can see what is meant when it is said that in documentary we get nearest to Pure Film. But from the actors' point of view I think the intellectual assumption that 'real' people, or as I would put it, 'non-actors,' are nearer to the truth than trained actors depends on what you mean by truth. Personally I feel, as Leigh Hunt did, that there is 'more truth in the verisimilitudes of fiction than in the assumptions of history' and, I would add, than in the documentation of that notorious liar, the candid camera.

I do not wish to seem to be flogging a dead horse. It is obvious that so-called 'real faces' have their place on the screen together with our numerous faces which are apparently real the first time you see them but which to my mind only become really interesting through the processes of the actor's art. I have often wondered what happened to the hero-actor of *Bicycle Thieves*. One hears that he was paid so much more money than he was earning as an artisan that his union ejected him on the grounds of his being a capitalist. Is it true, I wonder, that he attempted to get another job as a film actor and was told that since everyone associated him with his rôle in *Bicycle Thieves* he would never be credible in anything else, or did they discover that the only thing he could do was to live his part, and only live it once? Sorry as I am for him, I like to think either of these explanations is true. To lay bare one's innermost feelings is a necessity for the artist, it is part of his nature. For the other man it is degrading, both for him and for the art in which he is paddling. Actors are the only sincere hypocrites. Actuality has, of course, its appeal and its prescribed place on the screen. But *verismo*, the mingling of actuality and fiction, the dragging in of realistic detail as a kind of decoration, can become a pernicious business – we taste it and throw it up just as in certain novels and plays we spew up the autobiographical content when we feel it is not correctly fused with the creative. It is a special danger in films where it is so easy to set up a camera and see what happens. The mind behind the camera, which selects what it is going to shoot and then edits what is shot, must be the mind of the creative artist and the creative artist must, in order to achieve his effect of truth, control the perspective. Perspective is a form of distortion: It is the science or art of bringing three dimensions into the scope of two.

The actor must share this gift of perspective. He must persuade you that he is living his part while he is not. I dislike the candid camera not because it is unflattering but because my senses tell me it lies, as often as not. I dislike reportage for the same reason. There is of course the hundredth occasion when one or other tells an acceptable truth. The artist and the actor are not allowed so wide a margin of error.

NOTES ON DIRECTION

DIRECTING 'UNCLE HARRY'

This is an article I was asked to write for the enterprising little magazine 'New Theatre' (now, alas, defunct) on the production of 'Uncle Harry' at the Garrick Theatre in 1944 which was directed by William Armstrong and myself. Parts of it were used as the introduction to the Samuel French acting edition of the play.

'Who is Thomas Job?' So many people ask this that perhaps it is as well to state that to the best of my knowledge he is a Welshman, at one time a schoolmaster in Wales, who for the past twenty years has graced and kept warm the chair of drama in various American universities. It is by that much the less surprising that *Uncle Harry* should be hailed for what in its kind it is: a masterpiece of construction.

But, rare as well-constructed plays are, its success is due, one supposes, to something more than that. It is true that the most astute New York critic, John Mason Brown, who has seen both the American and English productions, attributes its success above all to its ingenuity, which is like that of a Torquemada puzzle, or a well-built machine, or, as he says, 'Algebra in wigs.' Its ingenuity is indeed amazing, and amazement does not lessen with acquaintance. But other critics have found in it a psychological depth which too seldom consorts with dramatic ingenuity, and a near-tragic pity and terror which, if not the classical catharsis of the emotions, are at least a recommendable detergent.

Uncle Harry, in its original version, was set on the English borders of Wales. It was first produced by American undergraduates. Later, on Broadway, it was given a French-Canadian setting. Now it has been repatriated and transferred by its present directors (who believed that actors could not compass the Herefordshire nor Shropshire dialect) to a North-country setting.

Here, there were two directors, William Armstrong and myself. Of our different functions there is no more to be said than that he was in on it before I was, and that I, acting in it as well as directing, have been with it longer than he has, that we share the responsibility for faults in the production and that whatever has been achieved could not have been achieved individually. It is, perhaps, worth remarking that such a collaboration is rarely practical, and demands not only identity of aim but complete mutual trust, as well as undivided loyalty from the actors.

We sat reading for a week.

However short the rehearsal period, whatever the play, at least one quarter of it should be spent sitting reading. For this reason: most bad or indifferent acting, like bad or indifferent writing, is made up of conventional tricks, banalities and clichés. Indeed it is hard to find a single performance on which such things do not at some time impose themselves. The most fertile ground for these clichés or banalities or tricks is self-consciousness. Self-consciousness is most evident in movement. To find the physical reality of a part requires the utmost concentration, and if this concentration is disturbed by groping for 'lines' the physical reality becomes broken up, uneven, and has to be patched together later. The same thing happens to what should be the unbroken line of thought behind the words. The continuous physical reality and the unbroken line of thought are of course interdependent, and the physical reality (and by this I do not merely mean 'moves') can dictate to the thought, but more often it is the other way round.

So we sat, read, marked, learnt and inwardly digested as much as we could in a week. We rehearsed for a month. We toured for two months, and during these two months we rehearsed some more, from time to time.

Our conception from the start was that this was a tragedy of circumstances, that the characters were conditioned by their economic station in a small town. It is important in almost any realistic play that the actor should be aware of the economic pressure on the character he is playing. But, although the author had intended the small town, we found, on closer examination of the text, that his intentions as to economic pressure were not precisely the same as ours. Harry, explaining the set-up to the commercial, says, in the text: '... The three children were left a legacy. Not much, but just enough to keep them in comfort if they lived together. Now mark that: *if they lived together!* You can see at once the situation a clause like that would create.' This can only mean that there was a clause in the parent's will requiring the three children should live together always. This gives the father a sort of Moulton-Barrett character to which there is almost no further reference, which is unnecessary to the plot and which, moreover, limits the cause of the tragedy to a kink of the parent. We have omitted the three words 'a clause like' and added later references to the Quinceys' insufficient income, hoping to suggest the not unfamiliar situation of a rent-free house and not enough money for Harry to set up a home of his own. Although to many people this seems to get across clearly enough, I wish very much that, without inventing a sub-plot, another character outside the Quincey household could be shown reacting to his economic circumstances, so that the implications of the situation would be inescapable. In a novel this addition could, I suggest, have been made with ironic force by the addition of a parasitic individual who was always willing to listen to Harry's story in order to get a free drink, and of whose ready sympathy Harry had become disgusted. But such an addition in the prologue would overbalance the play, and since the irony of the prologue is in any case savoured only at the end of the play, it would probably mystify overmuch.

The prologue is in any case overlong. For this I am responsible. Someone suggested that it would be more dramatic (in the strict sense) to see Harry's friends smile at him 'and cross to the other side of the road' rather than hear of it only as a prophecy from Lettie in the last scene. For this purpose I wrote in the entrance of the Glee Club and its new member in the Prologue. These two pages of dialogue undoubtedly contribute the intended effect in the end, but they are, I think, paid for at the time by the added mystification of the audience, and heavily by the actor who has to convey Harry's mildness and weak personality and at the same time spin an incredibly long yarn to a stranger. Perhaps this is the moment to confess also that there is no indication from the author that Harry is drunk in this scene, but it seemed to me that he might well have taken to drink and that drink might nerve him to tell his story. I have tried playing Harry as drunk and Harry as sober in this scene and I find, since in the theatre as in life a drunk is allowed to be a bit of a bore, that the audience more readily understands Harry in drink.

In the final scene in the Governor's office some people have objected to the improbability of the meeting of brother and sister in such circumstances. The scene was submitted to a legal authority and certain alterations were made. The Recorder of——, who has seen the play three times, says that such a meeting is by no means impossible and is quite acceptable to him and some of his legal friends. This is worth mentioning because of the number of people who, anxious to catch out the ingenious author (it is a tribute to him) maintain that such a meeting is unbelievable. In this final scene, Miss F. Tennyson Jesse, who took a great interest in the play, contributed some lines, notably the line of the hangman: 'Well, sir, the way I look at it is this: everyone in England is the executioner. I wouldn't be doing the job if the country didn't agree.' I added the horrible line about the length of the drop being nine feet, which, after asking Beatrix Lehmann her weight, I found from the Hangman's Ready Reckoner, printed as an appendix to that brilliant modern pamphlet: *A Handbook on Hanging* by Charles Duff.

It will be seen that, consciously or not, we have given to a modern work a mild dose of the 'Socialist-realism' which a Russian director would apply to any play, modern or classical. If the author had been on this side of the Atlantic, we might have succeeded in further intensification of our point of view, but we can only hope that Mr. Job, who clearly knows what he is about, will forgive our liberties with his text, and that if he does not, the success of his play will mollify his displeasure.

There were many other changes in the text, mostly due to our having to work from the Broadway script in which the setting was French-Canadian, but the above examples will serve to indicate the main shift of emphasis in the text itself.

But this was not the only shift of emphasis. The main shift was in the interpretation of the characters. Whether or not we have added anything of value to Mr. Job's script remains for an unprejudiced playgoer, when the text is printed, to decide.

Let it be clearly understood however that we have not altered anything for the sake of altering, nor for mere convenience, nor, I think, from failure to understand the author's intentions. Our first principle was to interpret the character in the light of the words.

To take three of the leading characters: it is clear that Harry must be (*a*) plausible, (*b*) capable of inspiring affection. This makes it perfectly clear to me that (*a*) he must be able to persuade himself as easily as he persuades others; that he has the liar's faculty of believing whatever falsehood he utters and that most of his lies are, as habitual liars' lies mostly are, half-truths; that, paradoxically, it needs considerable sincerity to be a successful hypocrite; (*b*) however horrible his character, his outward appearance, except perhaps at certain moments when he loses control, must be the reverse of crafty or sinister. Lettie must be more companionable than her sister Hester, yet equally dislikable. Conversely, Hester must be more frightening than Lettie, yet not entirely unsympathetic. Lettie, while doting on Harry, must be the strongest character of the three. Hester, while outwardly the most alarming, must be meet to be murdered, a born murderee.

Between these extremes, it can be seen, lies the extraordinary depth of these characters from the actors' point of view. The structure of the characters is very firmly made by the author, but the actors are left with unusual scope to develop them. This is not due, it must be stressed, to a weakness in the writing. On the contrary: in common with the great parts in dramatic literature, these three parts admit of a variety of interpretations.

Perhaps it would also be true to say that the fourth important character, Lucy, has extremes to reconcile which are almost as difficult and almost equally rich. There are lines to indicate that Lucy was of the type known as bossy, which partially explains why Harry, who wanted to escape the domination of his two sisters but who thrived on it nevertheless, picked her as the alternative, and why she picked him. From her behaviour in the first act she might almost be the type known as bitchy. But in the third act we have to see that the dominating factors are her ordinariness, her abundant common-sense and lack of imagination, and that she too is a victim, only a more lucky one, of her environment. Lucy requires to be played with as firm but even more delicate precision than the other three.

In some ways the character of Lettie is the most difficult in the play. The major hurdle is that the audience must be convinced, not only in the last scene but retrospectively, that any woman, condemned to hang tomorrow morning, would refuse the chance to live offered her by the man whom she has grown to hate and who is the real culprit. That no critic has ever questioned Lettie's decision to die is as much Miss Lehmann's achievement as the author's. The dialogue in this scene is considerably more rhetorical and theatrical than the bleak but characterful dialogue of the first two acts. It contains one touch of penetrating psychology, when Lettie says that as a child Harry would give his toys away as soon as he had broken them – 'and you'd act so generous, and everyone was expected to say how fine you were! And now you've broken your life and want to give that away! But it won't do, Harry, not this time.' This is fine. But it comes too late to help the previous scene, where Harry is supposed, after Lucy has refused him, to go to the piano and idly pick out the notes of a song, without any visible sign of emotion. I have tried playing this scene this way, but unless Harry is played throughout the play as unemotional and cold-blooded, it is incomprehensible. But to return to Lettie. By letting us see Lettie's obstinacy, her one-track mind, her lack of any sense of humour, her insensitivity to everyone's feelings excepting Harry's towards herself, her want of any kind of adult tact, her childish snatch-as-snatch-can tactics, her demands always backed up by the child's ultimatum of 'all-right-then-shan't-play,' her love of mischief, her contempt for all values other than those which obtain in Orchard Avenue, and especially her own home, by showing these things and by never deviating from her obsession, her 'super-objective,' which is to please herself by pleasing Harry, who is her faith, her religion, the actress in the first two acts gains command over the third. All these qualities in Lettie's character are to be found in the text, it is true, and very few extenuating qualities. How is it, then, that the character does not merely horrify? This is where performance ends and interpretation begins. Here is to be found the difference between acting and creative acting. Now some people think to have noticed that Lettie's love for her brother is what they describe as faintly incestuous. This, by their leave, is entirely due to some fixed idea which associates Miss Lehmann with two dramas of Eugene O'Neill. The little caresses and coy looks which Lettie bestows on Harry mean no more (and no less) than the similar blandishments which some emotionally under-nourished women bestow daily on their menfolk, from Bournemouth to Berwick-on-Tweed, embarrassing enough to visitors, and disturbing when shown frankly on the stage.

Whatever the name for it, it is not with this that Miss Lehmann makes Lettie her own creation, but by what one critic has been inspired to call a 'stale kittenishness.' The larky, jaunty, giggly, teasing, sighing, sniffing, sniggering schoolgirl which she presents is her own invention and in making this portrait she remains entirely faithful to all the author's intentions, but adds things which give the character a perspective and pathos which it might not otherwise have. We find that the Lettie of 1908 is the same Lettie who caught the tadpoles all those years ago and that her tragedy began long before the play started, before even her development was arrested, at the hands of the parents who would not consider that the children would ever be anything but 'the children.' When the light of her life goes out, we see the same character in the last scene, but in the shadow, as if the blinds of the sickroom had been drawn. To die tomorrow seems no great trouble to a woman who is in any case nearly dead.

Hester presents the same problem, in kind. Hester has almost no sympathetic traits. She is indeed a bully, and almost a senseless one. Her tyranny began as a child. It has become insatiable. She vents it not only on her household but on inanimate things. Like many whose lives are empty, she expends her energies in a futile, house-proud sense of order.

The additional horror is her enormous physical vitality. She is such a 'big, live woman.' That little Lettie and puny Harry should between them kill her has the same horror as when small animals contrive to kill a large prey. It strikes us as a reversal of nature, like the falcon in *Macbeth*, 'by a mousing owl hawk'd at and killed.'

Ena Burrill's success in this part is a striking testimony to the advantages of 'character acting' (as distinct from character-type-acting). Customarily cast for 'glamorous' young women of the world, Miss Burrill had to submerge every gesture, stance, tone of voice, which were native to her. Before applying make-up and wig and padding she had to find a new walk, a new voice, a new physical rhythm, and in addition the mannerisms typical to the character, such as the fidgeting adjustments of her clothes, which are always impeccably neat but whose folds and creases her obsession for order makes her constantly smooth and rearrange. Having established the physical reality of the character in this way, the actor or actress feels a sense of liberation. Just as amateurs or beginners feel happier as soon as they get into wigs or moustaches, behind which they can hide themselves, so the professional Miss Smith or Mr. Jones having 'lost themselves,' having lost their appearance and their own voice, lose also that surplus of exhibitionism which, until they come to terms with it, can vitiate all they do. This creation of an entirely new physical reality is a firm and comfortable base on which to play.

On this base, partly made by the actress and partly by the directors, a Hester grew who had a life of her own. Now the parts of this which were consciously made could be copied, but the parts which come from the subconscious (after the physical reality has been found) are entirely individual to Miss Burrill. It is the work of the subconscious which gives the final seal of quality to a performance. For this reason I believe that the first quality of a director (and I am speaking of the qualities which cannot be taught or consciously acquired) is an understanding of human relationships, and the second an understanding of the psychology of his actors, with the power to draw out of them the overtones, the quirks, the individual characteristics most suited to the character.

Now it is a simple fact that people with a good ear, or talent for mimicry, can mimetically reproduce something of the quality of voice of a great singer, whereas themselves are incapable of singing with more than average voice. In the same way that successful mimicking of another singing voice automatically impels a similar placing of the voice and more or less correct breathing, so the mimicking of the voice and mannerisms of a different physical type draws out, from the subconscious, something of the attitude of mind and behaviour of that type. Then when what we loosely call that type starts to speak the words of a character, surprising and exciting things happen. In this case Hester showed signs of a nervous disorder which, in spite of her strength, made her somewhat hypochondriac. Heavily armed for the offensive as she is, her clumsiness of mind and body makes her easily vulnerable. When she is wounded she starts to whine in the same way that bullies will. She becomes instantly the weakest of the family and we see that killing her is not so much a reversal of nature as we had thought. She is the weakest, and though we feel there is some justice in Harry's remark that 'it is better that two should die than three rot together,' our pity is stirred for Hester. I do not think, from the text alone, that one can find pity for Hester. The author supplies the terror, the actress the pity.

In a note (not in the text) the author says that Harry may be played either as the disappointed artist or as the ordinary, dilettantish amateur. The disappointed artist always seems to me the most prickly and unsocial of men and this interpretation of Harry would therefore be against the grain of the story, which is about a most ordinary and amiable man. I could wish that Mr. Job had been more explicit about Harry's emotional nature. I have already indicated some of my deviations from the Harry of the text. My suspicion is that Harry is intended by the author to be almost unemotional and cold-blooded. I admit to having imposed a certain hysterical strain on the character which is not in the text, at any rate not until the last scene. In the text there is no evidence of his hysteria except that he breaks a cup, sulks and that suddenly, on three occasions, he shouts, and once goes to the window for air. His symptoms of faintness, his tearfulness, stammering, his rather infantile mirth, and his dislike of being touched are superimposed. Not deliberately. They imposed themselves. They seemed to be necessary in view of the last scenes. As I have said, there is no indication in the verdict scene that Harry is overcome with hysterical laughter when Lucy turns him down. There is nothing except the words 'He breaks down,' to suggest the degree of his terror in the last scene. His last line: 'They say "murder will out!" But not my murder... My God, that's a good one!' is ironical just as all his lines, when Lettie has gone upstairs with the poisoned drink and while Hester is about to die, could be said with conscious irony. But such an interpretation never occurred to me until I heard an audience at Oxford ready to laugh during the murder scene as if the play were *Arsenic and Old Lace*. I should be intensely interested to see a version of the play in which Harry is played by a smaller man (Harry is supposed to be little) with complete, cold-blooded detachment. I think the play might be as exciting and probably much funnier. But I can't imagine what would happen in the last scene, and to my mind, unless the last scene convinces, this play cannot succeed. Somewhere between the two extremes, however, must lie a huge variety of interpretations.

I have spent all this space in discussing these three interpretations in detail in the hope of showing where the director's responsibility to both author and actors begins and ends, and it seems to me to point that if the author has written a complete and watertight play then the director and actors can set to sea in it without fear of sinking, and that, confident in his play, the author must have confidence in his crew to make the crossing, though they may visit uncharted coasts on the way.

Now for a postscript to these notes. *Uncle Harry* ran from early 1944 when we started touring it for E.N.S.A. to early the next year when, by previous agreement and also because of the wear and tear which such a rôle brings with it, I left the cast. The strain of any long run must be considerable but in a rôle such as Uncle Harry it became, to me at least, frightening. I used to inform the stage management of my whereabouts in the vicinity of the theatre some time before the call of the 'half-hour' when by general rule all of the actors must be at the theatre and at the 'quarter-hour' I would dash in, get into my clothes and dishevel my face for the opening scene where Uncle Harry is discovered in a state of maudlin drunkenness. When the final scene of sobbing hysteria was finished I seldom felt fit for anything. A sense of wellbeing became almost unknown to me in those days and all my energies save those required for the performance became dissipated and I often felt when meeting any but the most frivolous strangers that my personality was dissolving under their gaze. I was greatly helped at this stage by a psychiatrist who, after letting me talk for what seemed to me fifteen minutes but was in fact three hours, assured me in the most forceful tones that I was not, as I had feared, a subject for analysis.

But long before this state of personal disintegration set in, and which of course I do not assume was entirely due to the nature of the part and the length of the run, the general performance by the whole cast had altered considerably. The play and performances still made a considerable impact on the audience and it would have been difficult for anyone connected with the show to say precisely where it had changed. But it had changed and, most significantly, it now ran fifteen minutes longer.

My friend Norris Houghton had seen the play during the first weeks of its pre-London tour and returning from overseas saw it again in about its sixth month. He remarked at once that I was playing Harry in a much more neurotic manner than when I had started. I was unaware of this but at the next performance I could see that it was true. It occurred to me as the director that a similar shift of emphasis had perhaps infected the other performances to some extent. I was aware, even then, that actors, whether they have transformed themselves into a character or merely adjusted their personalities to approximate to a character, tend after a time to revert to type or, shall we say? to fall back on what comes most easily to them.

I called the whole cast for a rehearsal the following day and told them of the criticism which had been made of my own performance and of how I had judged it to be accurate. It seemed to me, I said, that there was no need to re-rehearse the entire play but that each actor must be prepared to make some small or large 'adjustment.' I carried in my hand Uncle Harry's Edwardian bowler hat and in it, as I informed them, were all their names on slips of paper, including of course my own. Before the names were drawn I explained that as director I would ask each one of them to go on the stage and act either in mime or with improvised words some scene which might be related to the play but which did not actually occur in it. I suggested to Beatrix Lehmann – the most co-operative of fellow-workers – that while she was waiting for her draw she should choose some moment 'outside the play' for me to improvise. Then before the improvisations began I told each member of the company where in my opinion his interpretation had altered (or reverted) and asked him whether he could see any truth in my guess. On the whole the company seemed to agree with me but I was not quite sure, with some of them, whether this might not be a wish to cut the cackle and end the rehearsal as soon as possible. However, they were all immediately intrigued as soon as the improvisations began, on themes which I had previously devised. A few of them were flummoxed and reports came back to me later, highly fantasticated of course but most amusing, of my 'high-falutin method'. Only the one member of the company who had flatly refused to believe that the performance had changed was totally unco-operative and gave an exercise like a sullen child who does not want to recite before the guests.

I remember that Beatrix Lehmann offered to be the first to improvise – a typically generous gesture – but I insisted that the names should be drawn from the hat.

The result was fascinating, for in nearly every case the improvisation was in tune with what the performance had become and that verdict was generally admitted to be true. The improvisation which Beatrix chose for me was that I should show what Uncle Harry did after the fall of the second act curtain when, having murdered one of his sisters, he shows the other that the blame will inevitably fall on her. After mildly remarking that that was precisely why the dramatist had let the curtain fall at that moment, I did my best by assuming that the surviving sister had fainted with fright at the news and I was left to ring up the doctor and the police which I did in tones of 'sincere' despair. Someone cheerfully objected to this on the grounds that Lettice, as played by Beatrix Lehmann, would never faint. But Beatrix, co-operative to the last, exclaimed 'Why shouldn't I?'

The performance that evening was twenty minutes shorter than its longest playing time and a minute faster than the first night. The audience was clearly gripped from the beginning to the end and for the first time in many weeks a few people let out a throaty and touching bravo.

'TIGER AT THE GATES'

APOLLO THEATRE, JUNE 1955

When the Giraudoux play 'La Guerre de Troie n'aura pas lieu,' which we played in England in Christopher Fry's translation known as 'Tiger at the Gates,' had been running in London for some time it was clearly necessary to call some kind of rehearsal. Mr. Harold Clurman, the director, had returned to New York where the production was to open in October 1955, and I took it upon myself to give notes to the cast. I also took the precaution of sending him a draft of what I was going to say to them, for I did not want him to think that I might have been giving the kind of notes which the leading actor sometimes gives, which can be less objective than those that the director himself might wish to give. As on the occasion of the rehearsal I called in mid-run for 'Uncle Harry,' which is described above, I was gratified to find that the whole performance pulled itself into a better shape and re-established the principles which Harold Clurman—one of the most remarkable directors I have ever worked with—had given to the production.

NOTES ON DIRECTION

This production has been moulded in a very firm shape by a very sure hand.

I am sure you all agree that the stylisation, rhetoric and long speeches of this play make it one which can more easily become set or hollow in meaning than a lot of other plays we could think of and I am going to suggest a few points which we should all bear in mind, not only for tonight's performance but for every performance.

One of the first things that happens when a play has been running some time is that the actors tend to forget the dramatic situation. We enter without being fully charged with purpose. We anticipate a turn of events. We ask questions in a tone of voice which shows that we know the answer. Sometimes, in fact often, this is only a matter of degree, a very small inflection. For instance, when Hector asks Busiris 'And what happened?' if I say it in a way which even faintly shows that Hector knows what happened, Busiris' reply is perceptibly less amusing. There are a great many questions in this play and only a few of them are purely rhetorical. In the first general scene – that is to say after the entrance of Priam and others – numbers of questions are fired back and forth, particularly at Hector. For instance, even the simple question of 'What do you see?' One might say that Priam is perfectly aware of what Hector is looking at; but there should be that note of wonder in his voice which shows that he does not know whether Hector is going to reply 'A goddess' or 'the moon' or 'the most beautiful woman in the world,' and without this note of wonder Hector's reply loses some of its effect. It is the same with Priam's opening question 'What did you say?' He knows perfectly well what Hector has said but he can scarcely believe it. Demokos' line 'He said he didn't care a fig about Helen' is all the more effective when it doesn't come too pat. And similarly with nearly all the questions in the play, including 'That was a new version of kiss you gave me. What was it?' The cure for all this kind of anticipation is listening, and listening as if every word that one hears is being said for the first time. This is what Stanislavski recommended an actor to do when he found himself not entirely inside his part. That is, to stop worrying about himself and listen to the other actors. It is an infallible cure; but it is something one should do all the time, every night.

That is anticipation of moment to moment. Anticipation of the end of scenes is even more damaging to a play because it signals to the audience what they are to expect and thus robs them of some degree of surprise and this can be cured by exactly the same means. In fact, if we listen to every word that is being said as if it were being said for the first time – and that can be done even when it is not being said in a particularly fresh manner – if that is done, anticipation whether small or large is automatically ruled out. In fact: *Look after the pence and the pounds will look after themselves.*

Now the question of entrances. Harold asked us once or twice to be ready for our entrances at least a minute before we go on and usually we are so. It doesn't always need a full minute of conscious work to prepare an entrance, but sometimes we come on, particularly when we are making a group entrance, forgetful of our purpose – that is to say, the reason why the dramatist has made that character enter at that particular moment. And the longer we play the easier it is to make what is in effect an automatic entrance. Fortunately for me, each of Hector's three entrances is very clearly defined. He is coming home to the wife he adores, a state of mind and body with which we are all familiar; he is determined to shut the gates of war and is expecting further bitter opposition; and he enters to interrupt Ajax because it is his business to see that there is no disturbance of the peace.

Let me take a few other entrances. The beginning of the first and the second acts are uncommonly difficult because of the way they are staged but I haven't any doubt whatever that they are effective and in each case it sounds to me as if you start the scene with a fine attack. Listening to the first scene I sometimes wonder if the attack is not a little too professional and if the cut and thrust between Cassandra and Andromache is not rather like an exhibition round by two experienced duellists. I think the cure for this is the same as for practically everything else; listening freshly and creatively. And I can't repeat too often that the more freshly you listen the more fresh will be what you say.

The entrance of the Old Men last night had lost its purpose and I did not believe that you were looking down at Helen any more than I believed that Cassandra and Hector were really looking down at the crowd. I have already spoken about the entrance of Priam and Demokos and the others but I think it would help Priam if he remembered that what has been said about him is that he is 'mad about Helen.' If that is remembered and coupled with the fact that he loves and admires his eldest son, the shock of hearing Hector's line will remove a suggestion of humorous tolerance which I think takes the edge off their first encounter. The Mathematician enters the play – or rather impinges on the audience – when he starts speaking and I have already suggested to him that he will find the right spur and freshness only by listening and that Hecuba's quip about 'Listen to the mathematician' should really give him a jet-propelled start because he hasn't really thought what he is going to say when he springs to the defence of Helen and says 'Anybody can tell you.' It is Hecuba who, by reminding him that he is a mathematician and scornfully suggesting that mathematicians know nothing about women, gives him his line of attack. Our actor anticipates Hecuba's quip nine times out of ten.

The entrance of the laundress and the other servant. I can only remind you of what Harold said to you more than once, and to be careful how you put that jug down.

The entrance of Helen is one of the most wonderful entrances any actress could ask for, but none the easier because of that. I suggest only that you remember the simplicity of the situation and not the difficulty of the entrance; that is to say, Helen is going to meet her brother-in-law, she hasn't yet been told a word about his opposition to her and she is anxious to meet this important and perhaps attractive man since all men are grist to her mill. I think if you remember this it will take away a slight feeling of self-consciousness which somehow communicates itself to the audience, as much as to say 'Look, here I am, chaps. This is what you've been waiting for.'

I have spoken to the Messenger about his entrance which is very difficult because of the nature of the set. Really he should have a good ten yards run in and he hasn't got it, but all the same, try not to creep out of the rocks. I wish to try cutting the messenger's second entrance which is an anticlimax after his first, and have written to Harold for permission.

The ending of the first act between the two girls is purposely written rather portentously and must be said with due weight but it sometimes sounds a little too portentous and I suggest that here too, the cure is to listen to each other as if you didn't know what on earth the other was going to say next.

There are two entrances in Act ii which are very important. It is everybody's concern that Busiris must be made tremen-

1947

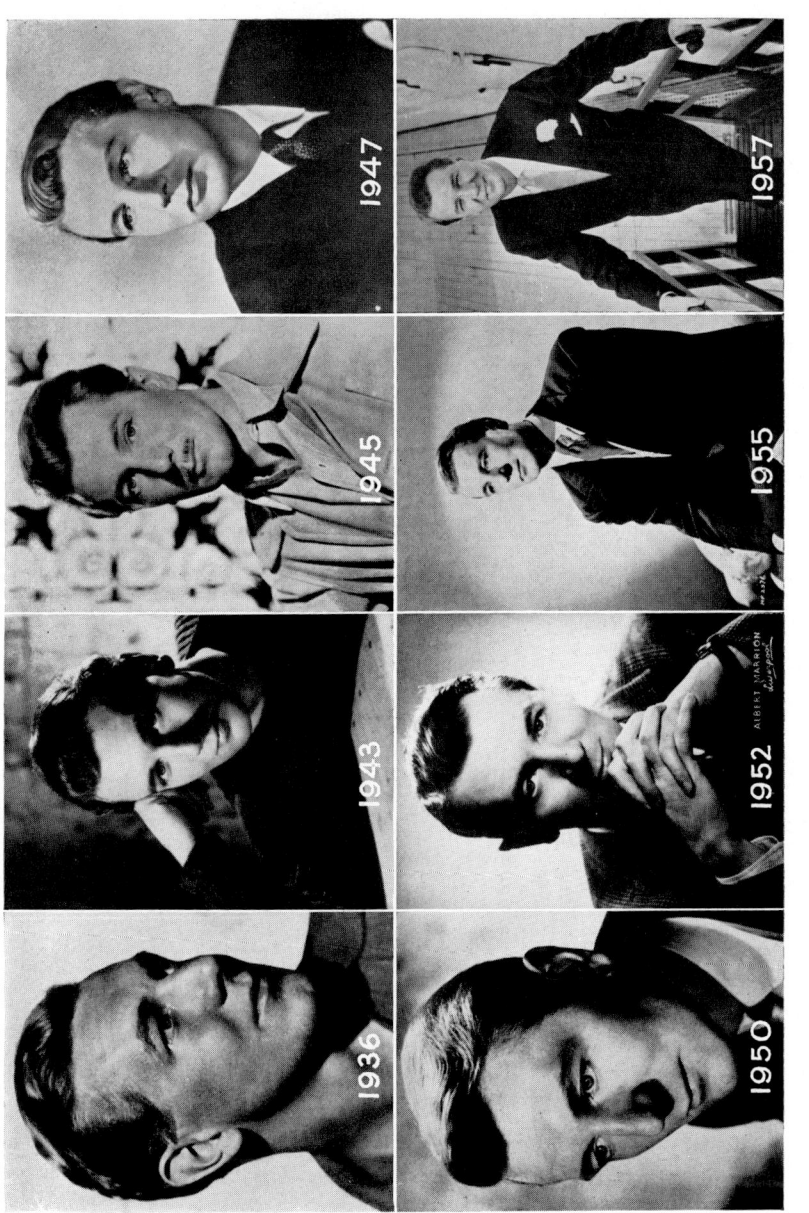

1957

1945

1955

1943

1952

1936

1950

'*Please send me a personally autographed photograph. I am 9½ years old and have seen all your films . . .*'

Prospero in *The Tempest*: Shakespeare Memorial Theatre, Stratford on Avon, 1951.

dously significant. The senators must watch him as far as it is possible to do so from the moment he appears. Presumably Demokos has told them of this trick he has up his sleeve and they must show by their faces that they are gleefully or maliciously anticipating Hector's discomfiture. On the occasions on which I have looked at the senators I have not known what they were thinking. Also, Demokos must not be too sure that his conjuring trick is going to come off; not anxious, but also not over-confident for that robs the entrance of suspense.

The news of the Greeks' arrival and later the entrance of the Greeks . . . Though the reaction here is stylised it must not be allowed to become too formal. Ajax's entrance with his two questions would get off to a flying start if he would remember to ask those questions as if they needed answering.

The sailors' scene is a very good example of how easy it is to slip into anticipating the result of the scene. The sailors are of course perfectly confident that what they saw was what happened. They trust their eyes. But they have against them two very important witnesses, Paris and Helen, and also the, I hope, not unimposing Hector, and they are only sailors compared to these great figures. It will make the whole scene much fresher if the sailors do not start off quite confident that they are going to convince everybody. 'Yes, and a rotten job you make of it' would help set the scene off if it was delivered with a note of astonishment – but *good humoured* astonishment. Try to remember that you are addressing Lord Louis Mountbatten. Until the sailors interrupt vocally they should not try to register by shrugs or whatever it may be their disbelief in what is going in, for that anticipates and thus weakens their own scene when it comes to be played. A look of blank astonishment would be much more suitable dramatically. Little things like pushing each other forward and back to corroborate each other could still do with a little work. The word 'seagull' is not always quite clear to everybody in the audience. Don't forget it's a surprising word. On the other hand, don't labour it. The same applies, by the way, to Andromache using the word 'heather' which needs to be picked out a tiny bit.

That is all for today. I have taken pains to sort these notes out to try and keep you for as little time as possible and I don't want to make a regular habit of giving notes just for the sake of giving them. But just as a famous Italian actor was known to say that the three requirements for acting were 'Voice, voice and then more voice,' so I will repeat until I am blue in the face that the three essentials which even the best and greatest actors need to keep in mind always, every night are: listen, listen and then listen again.

ECHOS DE CONSTANTIN

THE STANISLAVSKI MYTH

This was written in 1946 and is reprinted as first published.

IN THE THEATRE even Shakespeare abides our question. At least, some half-dozen of his plays abide unactable, or at any rate unacted. The only actors who escape question are those who escape notice. To find you have a critic who habitually seems to go out of his way to disparage you, or to come to hear now and then of some of the people who cannot bear you, simply cannot bear you, should really be a reassurance to an actor, although to be honest it never is. But here is one figure in the theatrical landscape which is the subject of such violent discussion, mystic adoration, wholly unreasonable dislike, or suspiciously lofty indifference, that it is hard to get people to look at the facts of the case. Stanislavski is quite high up in the tradition of Russian bogeys.

Opinions about Stanislavski as an actor are as various as is usual. There are those who say he mouthed and made faces. Myself, I do not see how anyone with such huge baroque lips could very well help mouthing. But all that is by the way. Whatever his qualities as an actor, he is known chiefly, and did I am sure wish to be known, as a man of the theatre, a director and the creator of an acting method which has exerted incomputable influence throughout the Western Hemisphere. Of his productions those of us who have not seen them must accept the judgment of those who did. Like the Irish Abbey players, many of the actors who worked with him before the revolution are scattered, though one catches occasional glimpses of them (Akim Tamiroff and Michael Chekhov, for example) in certain Hollywood films, where one longs to put them back into the setting to which artistically they belong. But even had not Stanislavski and Nemirovich-Danchenko's Moscow Art Theatre survived to this day as a living tradition and a contemporary force, we should still receive Stanislavski's influence through the pages of his book *An Actor Prepares* ...

Quite a few actors have, I know, read it and have found it immensely stimulating. Other actors have read it, and find it fairly frustrating. Some others again say they have read it when what they mean is that they have always meant to read it. Some have read of it and will, frankly have none of it. Some would sooner be seen dead than reading it. For all I know some may even have died reading it. Very few have read it again.

It is because I have read it again several times and because I find myself returning to it that I am writing this. But first let me continue in a personal vein for a little. I have written about it once before, and I find that to become identified with a subject about which there is misunderstanding and prejudice is to invite these things on oneself. I do not mind being greeted with 'Hello, Stanislavski,' or 'Hi-ya Konstantin' or receiving anxious enquiries as to the state of my 'super-objective' or whether 'my units' are in order. Only my friends dare do this and in any case it is not unflattering.

What is not so satisfactory is when people suppose that I would mean my own work to be an example of the Stanislavski method, or assume that I would condemn any style of work which is not based on his method. For of course no single actor could possibly, on his own, give any effective demonstration of the method. This can only be done by a group, and would take years to perfect. As far as I know, the only English-speaking group which has attempted to absorb and put the method into practice has been the Group Theatre of New York, who were seen here only in *Golden Boy*. (Alas, the Group Theatre is also now disbanded, and the better known members of it are known here only through the screen: Luther Adler, Morris Carnovsky, Clifford Odets, John Garfield). But I have derived great stimulus from the book, and constant reference to the high standards it demands can help check, to some extent, the varying quality of one's work. When I have directed plays I have tried to apply its first principles; that is to say I have tried to dissuade actors from flying at their parts 'like French falconers,' hoping to give a performance at the first rehearsal, and to try to make sure that they supply themselves with a good imaginative foundation to the part.

For again and again we see actors who start off well but who can never give a full expression of the character because they have not imagined it fully and actively and laid its foundations well; or others who have given a good performance on the opening night, while their imaginative powers were still at work, but who gradually lose life and conviction as the run proceeds, repeating maybe each move and inflection with expert precision but finding that they need the stimulus of a 'good house' or 'someone in front,' or a particular scene in which they know they are especially effective to help them give their best. They are aware that something has gone out of their performance, but they do not know what it is. They know that certain scenes become increasingly difficult to play and they do not know why. At worst, they begin to indulge in private jokes which even the audience can see are not part of the play. Even the actor will have recognised some if not all these symptoms in his own or other actors' work. Nor are these flaws primarily caused by long runs. They are caused, quite simply, by the actors losing sooner or later (some lose quite early) the 'offered circumstances,' on which their part, not to mention the plot, depends.

Every actor knows how the impact of a first night audience adjusts his sense of the play as a whole. Some less thorough actors are never so good as on opening nights. The audience reactions supply such actors with the impulses which should have come earlier. But although audiences vary they do not vary to the extent of supplying a fresh stimulus every night, and then such actors become morbidly dependent on their audiences and cannot give their best except on rare and unpredictable occasions. Such actors need to go back to the beginning and start again, trying to revive that imaginative faculty of believing in what they are doing. For that is part of what Stanislavski taught: belief. No half-belief. Not make-believe. Belief that does not begin and end by an intellectual process, but which is so deep-rooted that it fires each movement, echoes in each silence, and penetrates beyond 'the threshold of the subconscious,' where it becomes creative...

The best short summary of the Stanislavski method is to be found in Norris Houghton's admirable *Moscow Rehearsals* which prospective and past students of the method would do well to get from the library. As Houghton says: 'The Stanislavski system is really only a conscious codification of ideas about acting which have always been the property of most good actors of all countries whether they knew it or not. Its basis is the work of the actor *with himself* in order to master "technical means for the creation of the creative mood, so that inspiration may appear oftener than is its wont" ' ...

It is not my purpose here to re-examine or condense the system. But I would like to sweep away one or two of the prejudices which ignorance and fear have created round that thunderclap of a name: Stanislavski.

Fear? Yes, where some actors are concerned. For there are those who feel that the very existence of this book implies some criticism of their own achievements and acting experience. Well, it does and it doesn't. It doesn't, for the reasons Houghton gives above. It does, I think, because there is no actor or actress living or dead who could sincerely read this book and not find some chink for doubt if not despair. Do actors despair? Only actors will understand that use of the word. Some actors even will not, those who sublimate their despair, their essential lack of 'actual reality,' the substance, the essence, the nature or 'the thing' which makes them actors, the hellish, or divine, doubt which drives them to live more thoroughly others' lives than their own, to haunt, as it were, their own existence.

'A job is a job,' they say. 'Less of this talk about art.'

But I digress; the actor's temperament is something which need not be more than hinted at here. If an actor can master the self-criticism which reading *An Actor Prepares* will bring he has gone some way towards the reconciliation of such doubt. He may go further, he may effect a reconciliation with his own exhibitionism, that quality in every actor which none can lose without losing the desire to act, but with which somehow or other he must come to terms, to the point at least of knowing when he controls it or when it is controlling him.

I have said it is likely he will receive some shocks to his self-esteem but for these he is more than recompensed by the startling corroboration and, be it stressed, simplification of many of his own vague and fluctuating ideas and feelings about his craft. It is a truism to say that acting cannot be taught. Certainly no book can teach anyone to act. But no one would deny for a moment that to come in close contact with a great actor working at his craft must be illuminating, and to read *An Actor Prepares* is to be privileged to be in close contact with a great actor-director not in 'a fiction and a dream of passion' but in the great evening of his life, still in active contact with what is probably the greatest of living theatres, telling us again and again, with all the clarity of a great intellect, the simple truths of our art.

Foremost among these is the dictum that our three masters are 'feeling, mind and will,' that feeling comes first but can never effectively operate without the other two. Many great actors have arrived at much the same verdict; notably Talma, who insisted that 'sensibility and intelligence' are the two indispensable qualifications for acting: sensibility, the power to apprehend emotionally the entire content of character and action; and intelligence, the power to reduce that emotional experience to a technical formula which can be repeated at will. Sensibility cannot be consciously acquired, which is why acting cannot be taught. Intelligence, one might say, is the power to see the relationship of things, the power to keep these relationships in perspective. Stanislavski's book is like some great mirror, wherein a man can see, standing close to the glass, the first mirrors of his soul, his own eyes, and in them, the tiny shape of the surrounding countryside; standing further back, he sees his setting reduced into a frame, and somewhere in that frame, looking curiously impermanent, the figure of himself. But of course the mirror can only reflect what the man can see for himself. All it constitutes is a sense of nearness, a sense of distance, a relationship, some proportions. For to read *An Actor Prepares* is like going on a trip abroad: a man can receive from either experience only in proportion to what qualities he brings with him. But to read it at all implies some degree of serious respect for his craft and whatever else he finds in it, the actor-reader will receive the most sustaining reassurance that has yet been put on record that his work can at its best be creative and achieve not merely réclame, but dignity. It will probably make him profoundly dissatisfied with the conditions of work prevailing in this country. All the better.

And for audiences? I find it hard to imagine that any but the most ardent amateurs of acting will find the patience to read the book. It would be worth their pains. It would perhaps induce them to try to distinguish between the actor and his part, a distinction seldom made by audiences, rarely by critics even. It might help them to realise that the abiding necessity for every actor, as for every artist, is the avoidance of cliché, the easy, effective, conventional mode or trick of self-expression. Cliché is like a weed: no garden is free from it all the time. The greatest performances are those which are most free from it, those in which every detail has been freshly conceived and which retain at each performance enough of that freshness. It is this freshness which contributes whatever is most exciting and at the same time satisfying in the theatre.

To take an extreme example: 'He dies,' says the stage direction. How every amateur actor loves to find that he is to die on the stage! At once he sees himself as the centre of all eyes (correctly, as often as not). And yet, however heavily foreshadowed in the action, death on the stage must come, as it comes in life, as a shock: 'Can he be, is he, really, dead?' He is, or he is not, and it is not the inert, still body that proclaims the actor dead; as often as not we do not believe it much, but divert our attention to what follows. If we did not know Olivier to be a great actor by other tests we should know it from the manner of his deaths. Each one is in character. His Macbeth died violently, convulsively, as he had lived, but in spite of his defiant last words we knew that he had lost heart. His Richard III had no heart to lose and fought on and on, his muscles still twitching when all sense had left them. In the death of his Hotspur is all the essential simplicity and wonder of that character, and its rough and ready philosophy; we are made to feel, most poignantly, the surprise and astonishment of a brave, headstrong young man cut off in his prime.

As with death, so with a thousand other commonplaces of life and of the theatre: an embrace; a hasty entrance; the light shock to which we react quickly; the deep shock which our feelings, in order to protect us, at first reject; the manner of starting a quarrel; the manner of saying a long farewell. When these things are well and truly acted they seem simplicity itself. 'But,' says the reader, like the student in Stanislavski's book, 'all this is obvious!' To which his master retorts: 'Did I ever say it was anything else?' Yet how often do we see these simple truths really convincingly performed? Do not a great many audiences prefer, or at least feel more comfortable when witnessing, the artifices and the clichés to which they are accustomed? Many prefer to see the wheels going round. They would often rather see an actor 'acting' acting, which I suppose makes them feel they know where they are, than acting the part without concession to convention. I feel this to be so and do not see how it could well be otherwise, since in any art the conventional is the most popular. But just as for an actor to give himself up to conventional acting will in time dry up whatever imaginative powers he may possess, so it is with audiences; they become lazy, bored and only the most violent stimuli will satisfy them.

Hence, amongst other things, the appetite for 'pace' for its own sake, to which must be sacrificed one of the essentials of any artistic performance, rhythm.

There are in England today, roughly speaking, two styles of acting: the acting in which the effect springs from the cause, and that which begins with effect and which rarely, and only in part, seeks the cause. The latter style is still very much the preponderant. It is very seldom we see a production in which more than a few actors are faithful to the author, the director and their artistic conscience.

'Always he sought,' said Nemirovich-Danchenko, 'the essence of the play in the times and events described; and this he expected the actor to understand. This is what Stanislavski called the core, and it is this core which must stir the actor, which must become part of him for the time being.' Our most-read dramatic critic holds that great acting is achieved in a 'blaze of egotism.' I personally doubt if this was ever an accurate description of a style of acting which is going out of fashion, a fact of which he is aware but which he chooses to disregard, holding that this age's failure to produce such performers is due to the decadence of the time rather than, as I believe, an inevitable and healthy change in taste. Nowadays our aim is for a theatre of synthesis, not a synthetic theatre. Some of us think that there are heartening signs that we may one day achieve such a theatre.

If you think all that sounds a dull proposition, then the great Russian actor's methods and books are not for you. There will always be plenty of 'egotism' smouldering away somewhere, so you pays your money and takes your choice. But blazing or smouldering, it is consuming itself, leaving the maybe highly-talented egotist to eke out what remains of his or her power in a succession of similar displays or revivals of former successes, until finally there is no capacity, no urge left to explore; the fire has become a formula. If the talent is a great one it will see them through, but they will have contributed only a token payment of the debt which great talent owes. By loving themselves in art and not the art in themselves they have, paradoxically enough, left much of their art unused. It is one of the virtues of Stanislavski's method that it encourages actors not to let this happen. It is one of the faults of our system, in which actors are casual labourers, that it happens far too often.

STANISLAVSKI AND BRECHT

The editors of 'World Theatre' had the agreeable notion in 1954 that it might help to clear up some of the violent confusion then current about Bertolt Brecht and his Epic Theatre if some of the leading actors from most of the European countries were asked to make some comparisons between his theories and those of Stanislavski who, roughly speaking, might be said to be the direct opposite. So far as I know, only Jean-Louis Barrault and myself contributed anything to this symposium. I have not altered this article either.

No one system or method of acting contains or can contain all of acting. One of the great merits of the Stanislavski Method is that it contains more of acting than any other. It may leak a little but, nevertheless, not only does it contain more but it has exerted tremendous influence and like all powerful ideas it lends strength to those who oppose it.

It is no new thing to oppose Stanislavski. Meyerhold started that long ago and, though his 'bio-mechanical' method may not correspond exactly to the Brecht theory, I strongly suspect that so far as the *acting* was concerned, a competent jury would not be able to distinguish between a typical Meyerhold production and a typical production by Brecht. Since I have not seen a production by either perhaps this will be thought unfair, even foolish. Certainly I do not mean to be disrespectful to either. Both are men of theatrical genius, both rebels, both – and this is significant – appealing to mass audiences. There is little or nothing wrong, in theory, in appealing to mass audiences. But, as Hollywood discovered long ago, what you offer mass audiences must be in some manner pre-digested, like patent breakfast food. In Hollywood, by and large, it is 'pre-digested' by removing any trace of social comment except the comment of cliché. In Brecht, the matter, the substance, is certainly not so much pre-digested as rammed into the audience, just as Bernard Shaw rammed home his ideas, though to a different kind of audience than those of Hollywood or Brecht, by didacticism and rhetoric.

I said the Stanislavski Method leaks a little. Let me make it clear that in my opinion it still floats, and floats superbly when in the right waters. Where in my own experience I think it founders is when it is applied too rigidly to the works of dramatists such as Shakespeare. I say too rigidly, for we must remember that the chief purpose of Stanislavski's Method is to help the actor to recapture at will the creative mood. But despite Salvini and his Othello – which again, obviously, I never saw – despite also Stanislavski in his book on producing *Othello*, I find that in my own experience one can only use a very small part of the Stanislavski Method in preparing or acting the great rôles of Shakespeare. It is of very little use for Macbeth or for Richard II, or for any of the parts in which there are apparently irreconcilable elements. These elements are reconciled not so much by the actor as by Shakespeare and the actor's attempts to aid him defeat their purpose. For example, I agree completely with Bernard Shaw on the subject of Lady Macbeth:

'If you want to know the truth about Lady Macbeth's character, she hasn't one. There never was no such person. She says things that will set people's imagination to work if she says them in the right way: that is all. I know: I do it myself.'[1]

I fully realised the wisdom of this when I came to play Prospero in *The Tempest* for the second time. Prospero must be one of the most irreconcilable great parts in literature, but Shakespeare reconciles him by Ariel, by Caliban: the light and dark sides of man's nature, the spirit, and the flesh; just as he reconciles King Lear by Kent, Edgar and the Fool, all parts of Lear. (In the middle section of *Lear* are the greatest scenes for 'group' acting ever written.) If and when I play Prospero again I will use only this one, fanciful memory of Stanislavski: I will wish that Stanislavski might be alive to play Prospero himself; I will imagine him wishing to 'break his staff' and 'drown his book,' not bidding farewell to his art (as people like to fancy Shakespeare was doing when he wrote this, his last play), but to 'retire to Milan,' or rather to Stanislavski's beloved Moscow

[1] *Bernard Shaw and Mrs. Patrick Campbell: Their correspondence.* Edited by ALAN DENT. (Victor Gollancz Ltd, 1952.)

and then in all his wonderful humility to start again, telling us what, in conclusion, he finally meant, simply and briefly, and sparing us all the books and pamphlets and old lectures which are promised us still from Russia. Constantin Sergevich knew how to be simple but it is in the nature of a long life and a great mind not to be brief, and the seemingly endless stream of posthumous publications promised us may only add to the existing confusion about this great master.

I do not understand all of the article on and by Brecht which has been sent me. The basic ideas are not new to me for I have followed Brecht at a distance with sympathetic interest for some time. One cannot help comparing his didacticism with that of Shaw, for, like Shaw or all didacticists, he does not scorn any over-statement that will serve his ends. I think I see what he is after, in fact I am sure I do, but his over-statements confuse me. Of course it is very tempting, when a man of even such brilliance confuses you, to suppose that he is himself confused. One does not wish him to be an aphorist but one expects him to shed light. To me, Brecht sheds light as cars do at cross-roads at night. But, as I say, I think I see clearly enough where he is going.

I think we should disregard his occasional rudenesses and his occasionally almost childish attempts at logic which result in too many a *reductio ad absurdum*. Nevertheless, it is not easy to ignore some of them. His comment on the remarks of the great Danish actor Paul Reumert, when he (Brecht) says that to make an audience think it sees a rat when there is no rat (Reumert's example) is to produce an effect like making the audience drunk with alcohol; that is not merely rude but plainly silly. To compare the illusions of art with the illusions of drink would be infantile, except that no infant would think of comparing the two. His theory of the historic past makes me rub my eyes in bewilderment. Can he, I ask myself, really be talking the language of reason or even common-sense? Doggedly I go over his words again and I have, reluctantly, to decide that if I am to retain my sanity I must decide that this genius has here lost his. For the idea that any moment in history is isolated from its past or its future and that this idea can be communicated in a performance is something that verges on the insane. I must assume therefore that Brecht does not really *mean* it and that, like so many of his other juxtapositions and paradoxes, he uses it just as a defending or opposing Counsel may use such things in a Court of Law: knowing that they will not be fully believed, but content that they shall sway the judgment of the jury.

Assuming that his theory has at least some validity, some of his paradoxes are understandable. His double invoice of what is demanded of the 'Dramatic Theatre' and, in the other column, of his 'Epic Theatre' is here and there to be understood, whether one sympathises with all of it or not.

Again, in what play can it really be said that in *Dramatic Theatre* 'man is unalterable' and in *Epic Theatre* that man is 'alterable and altering?' Here we get near the knuckle. For, superficially, there might seem to be some truth in this. But the distinction is so fine that it is at best forensic. The implications of, shall we say, *King Lear*, are that it is foolish for fathers to behave so, and wicked of some children to react so. No one assumes that all fathers behave so, should behave so, or would behave so. The very simple-minded may think so, but it is not so. *King Lear* has a general, not a literal, truth.

But I am ready to believe that Brecht is not the first or the last master whose practice does not always square with his precepts. One Anglo-American critic, Eric Bentley, a fervent and penetrating admirer of Brecht and his plays, has said as much in his book *The Playwright as Thinker*.[1]

Stanislavski always insisted that his Method was little more than a conscious codification of germinating impulses and ideas which all really good actors and actresses had found and find for themselves instinctively. If only the actors and actresses who are frightened of Stanislavski would remember this!

Brecht is more aggressive. It is the nature of rebels to be so. He is also, I suspect, more egoistic. Most actors are familiar with that old story: 'It is good for the actor to be *shown how to act his part*.' He covers this nonsense up by suggesting that 'another actor' *or* 'the producer' should act as demonstrator. But it is a hollow pretence and, with respect, I suggest that he does not realise how much of Bertolt Brecht is Echt Ego.

I am inclined to credit the British producer and the British actor whom I have questioned on the effect of Brecht's theory in performance. Both are masters of their craft and both speak German fluently. They seem to agree that Brecht's actors, like other companies of actors, vary in excellence, but that the best performers seem to be just like the best performers in other companies and other countries.

Be that as it may, it is much to the credit of Brecht that *World Theatre* should have considered this controversy a profitable one. We shall not know many of the answers until, just as Stanislavski's productions are still played in Russia, we find whether Brecht's plays and productions are still played, in forty or fifty years' time, in Germany. I will rashly prophesy that the plays may be. I assume that it is part of Brecht's theory that the productions will no longer be suitable for that time.

[1] Reynal and Hitchcock, New York, 1946.

EPILOGUE

THE OTHER ACTORS have left the stage, the curtain is about to fall, and Prospero, the old magician, steps forward:

> Now my charms are all o'erthrown,
> And what strength I have's mine own,
> Which is most faint...

Like Prospero's words, this brief epilogue to a book is something half-way between a wish and a prayer.

I wish, of course, that anything I have said which may sound dogmatic should be taken with the necessary pinch of salt. Most of what I know or guess with any certainty I can only act. The little which I am able to put into some sort of words does not, in essence, take long to say, and most of that I have said before. I am content to go on asking questions, provided that some of these are the right questions.

The actor does not have to act all day long, but from the moment he wakes till the time he goes to bed he must be prepared to act, and act to the best of his powers. Life is too short for the actor not so prepared. The only times when he is not ready and able to do this must be the times when he is on holiday, deliberately taking a pace back in order to make a longer leap. These can be magical, restoring times, when the body gathers strength and the mind lies fallow. If he is successful he will be tempted, at the height of his powers, to take on more than he should; especially in these days, when the public has so many distractions ready to hand; when films and records,

EPILOGUE

photograph-sittings and brief television appearances are, by former standards, so painless to perform and sometimes ludicrously lucrative into the bargain. He may even, if he likes putting words together and can wield a pen or dictate to a secretary or operate a tape-recorder, write a book. If he does, he will hope that it will be understood that he is an amateur in this field. He must understand that whatever he writes will not change anyone's opinions of his acting powers. Nor should it. Whatever he has when the lights are on and the curtain is up is all that he has in the eyes of the world. His better qualities as a human being, however benevolent or shrewd, and his worser, ranging from the vain to the petty and ridiculous or still worse, are only to be valued, and will only be remembered, insofar as they are reflected in his performances. 'The readiness is all . . .'

But even the more successful men have moments when they must feel despair, as Irving must have felt it when his wife asked him, as they drove home after the first of his great triumphs, whether he intended to spend the rest of his life making a fool of himself in public. At this moment Irving stopped the brougham, stepped out and never returned home nor spoke to his wife again. The wisdom of that decision far outweighs its apparent ruthlessness.

At such moments actors, and other men, may well choose to remember Molière. In the last hours of his final, fatal illness, during which he had been writing, of all things, *Le Malade Imaginaire*, Molière was asked if he would not receive the last sacrament, denied in those days to actors, whose very profession automatically excommunicated them from the Church. He had but to renounce his calling, as most of his colleagues felt compelled to do in their last minutes of life.

The Comédie-Française, called also the Théâtre Français and, sometimes, in honour of France's great actor-dramatist, La Maison de Molière, still rocks with his life's laughter. His presumed birthplace in the Rue St. Honoré is now a butcher's shop. His grave remains unknown.